THE DABOVICH FAMILY TREE
SAVO (SAM) DABOVICH---GRANDFATHER
CHRISTINA DABOVICH------GRANDMOTHER
CHRIS DABOVICH------------FATHER
EUSTOLIA DABOVICH-------MOTHER
NIKO DABOVICH--------------UNCLE
DANITZA SABOVICH---------AUNT
EVA SZMARDICH-------------AUNT
ZORA VUKASOVICH---------AUNT

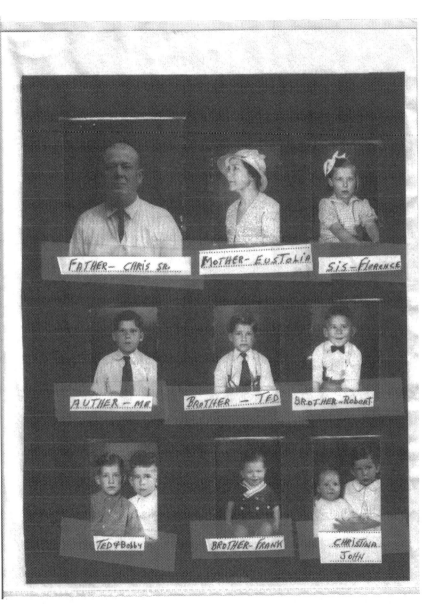

CHIHUAHUA HILL

Bisbee, Arizona

CHRIS DABOVICH

iUniverse, Inc.
New York   Bloomington

CHIHUAHUA HILL
Bisbee, Arizona

iUniverse books may be ordered through booksellers or by contacting:

*iUniverse
1663 Liberty Drive
Bloomington, IN 47403
www.iuniverse.com
1-800-Authors (1-800-288-4677)*

*Because of the dynamic nature of the Internet, any Web addresses or links contained in this book
may have changed since publication and may no longer be valid.*

*ISBN: 978-1-4502-3701-7 (sc)
ISBN: 978-1-4502-3702-4 (ebk)*

Printed in the United States of America

iUniverse rev. date: 2/17/2011

AUTHORS NOTES

I have so many people that I am grateful to for helping to get my book published;

My sister Christina LaChance for typing my messy scrawl into her typewriter and correcting my grammar.

My son Chris III, for giving me "tips and other secrets" to writing.

My wonderful Granddaughter Haley for continuing to inquiring what I was going to write about.

My wife Christina, for having the patience to put up with me and my lack of it!

And lastly, Delrena Dabovich for putting the finishing touches on, retyping and submitting my manuscript to the publisher.

All played an important part in the completion of my book.

Thank you,

Chris Dabovich II

The early morning smelled of chorizo. People on Chihuahua Hill, a neighborhood of houses clinging to the face of the mountain in this quiet mining town in Bisbee, Arizona, were getting out of bed and eating breakfast. Which consisted of mostly chorizo with eggs or chorizo "con papas."

Chorizo is a mixture of ground beef and pork, with powdered hot red chili, oregano and other spices. The chorizo was put in a skillet and cooked with eggs, which were added at the precise time and scrambled. It was and still is a very common, tasty breakfast in the communities of Mexican origin. At times, to break up the monotony of chorizo and eggs, the lady of the household would substitute potatoes for eggs, thus creating "chorizo con papas." Everyone in Southeastern Arizona and Northern Mexico enjoyed this wonderful cuisine.

It was the early part of June in the year 1944. I was awakened by two voices outside my bedroom window. The clock in my bedroom read a little after seven o'clock in the morning. I got up and peeked out through my opened window. There, three men on the concrete landing along the side of our house. Two of the men were digging on the landing. The third man looked on. "Hecha otro valde de aqua a escusado", yelled the man who looked like he was a supervisor. The order was directed at a woman who was standing on her porch, three houses above ours. In translation, he was telling the woman to pour another bucket of water in the toilet. The men were trying to unplug a sewer main, which served the houses on Chihuahua Hill. Again, the sewer boss hollered at the old lady, "Otro valde, por favor", ("another bucket, please".) The old lady, apparently hard of hearing, yelled, "Que dici?" ("What does he say?") The women's small granddaughter, about nine years old, stood at the top of the stairs and told her grandmother, that the men wanted another bucket of water poured into the toilet. "Ah,

1

bueno," replied the old lady, as she disappeared into her house. "Ya esta bien," yelled the City boss toward the house. He then directed his voice to the two men and said, "Okay boys, the shit's rolling now, this sewer line is open. Fill the hole and I'll see you guys back at the warehouse" I made my bed, took a shower and got ready for what was ahead of me on this particular Saturday.

In the kitchen my mother was busy making pan cakes for breakfast. Her name was Eustolia and she was born in Sinaloa, Mexico and came to the United States with her mother in 1910. She was a very unique person. She could do about anything. She was good at house repairs, housework, sewing, gardening, just about anything put before her. She learned and wrote English by reading "The Bisbee Evening Ore"."Good morning, son", she said. I replied, Mom loved to go to Bingo games. In fact, all her evenings were dedicated to Bingo. When she went to Bingo, she would play one card, just one, all night long. I asked her one day, "Why don't you play more than one card and your chances of winning are greater." She replied, "You only win with one, Son." Mom could really cook. All her meals were from scratch. Our Thanksgiving Day meal was the best I have ever eaten, bar none! She was quite a lady. Sadly, she is no long with us.

Anyway, like I said previously after getting up and coming in the kitchen, I greeted my mother with, "Hi mom, did you sleep well last night? Where's Pop?" "He went to the store for Baba," replied my Mother. Every morning my dad would go check on his mother. My dad's mother, whom we all called Baba, was in her early nineties, but well preserved. She was of a medium build, but strong, very strong for a woman her age. She looked like the women you see in Geographic Magazine. She wore a shawl, was fair with red, red cheeks. She had a very pretty smile. My dad's father, whom we called Yedo, had died about eight years earlier, so Baba was all alone in her big house. By the way, in the Serbian language, Baba means "Grandmother" and Yedo means "Grandfather."

Both of my grandparents, on my dad's side, had been born in Vienna, Austria. Neither bothered learning the English language all the time they lived in Bisbee. However, my dad learned both English and Spanish, along with his native Serbian language. He spoke the three languages fluently. As a matter of fact, my dad worked as an interpreter at the Cochise County Court House whenever there was a case involving Hispanics that didn't understand the English language.

My Dad was born in Vienna, Austria. He came with his parents to the United States at the age of eight. It wasn't long before he was speaking English as well as Spanish, plus all the slang and dirty words in both languages. He leaned quickly while hanging around boys his own age. He did not want us to speak his Serbian language as we were growing up. He would tell my sister and me, "We are living in th United States and we will all talk in English." We said "Okay," and let it go at that. However, we lived in a Mexican neighborhood. The kids spoke Spanish as well as English, so we did also.

My sister, Florence who was about a year and two months older than me, came into the kitchen and said, "Good morning Mom." My mother replied, "Good morning dear, sleep well?" "Yes," answered my sister, "I slept well, thank you. I'm going to take a really quick shower, cause I have to work in another hour and a half." My sister was a telephone operator for a Mountain Bell system. Her place of work was about a five minute walk from our house. Florence had been a telephone operator since she was a freshman in high school. She was a junior now. She would go to school, come home, change clothes and go to work until nine o'clock at night. Aft school was out for the summer, she would work eight hours a day like the other ladies. What salary she made, she kept for herself to buy clothes, costume jewelry, lipstick, nail polish and whatever young girls buy at that age.

At this particular point in my life, I was seventeen and would be eighteen in six months. I was going to start my senior year at Bisbee High School, but for now I was more interested in going to town to see what was going on. There were always guys hanging around. I'd go there, tell a few jokes, look at the girls, etc. Sometimes we, (the guys and I) would get together to play a baseball game. We use to play a lot of baseball n those days. Everyone had a glove, bats and balls. These were the names of the teams: The Chihuahua Hill Indians, The Tin Town Rats, The Warren Pretty Boys, The Don Luis Bastards and The Brewery Gulch Gangsters. I lived on Chihuahua Hill, but played on The Brewery

Gulch Gangsters team. Why? I guess it was because most of the guys I palled around with were on the Gangsters team.

My Dad had ordered a burro load of dry mesquite wood. Mr. Encinas had a herd of burros and he delivered wood to most of the families that burned wood used for cooking and heating. The load would be unloaded at the bottom of the concrete steps or the sidewalk, Since everybody bought wood, we had to get our load up to our house before someone would steal it. I had a chopping axe and it was my job to cut the long lengths into small enough pieces to fit in our stove. I did not mind chopping wood for our family. I took it for granted that all kids helped their parents this way. It would be many years later that I would learn that the majority of kids didn't help around their house. In the long run, I'm glad I was brought up the way I was. It helped me later on in life. It made me self reliant, helpful and I leaned not to be lazy. I thank my father and mother for that. Once in a while a railroad car full of coal, for the Independent Fuel and Feed Company would come into town for the man who sold it to the town. My dad would help unload the coal from the railroad car. When the job was done, my brother Ted and I would take a couple of gunny sacks, fill them with small pieces of coal, the size of walnuts and take them home. The coal would fit just right in our stove. It was cleaner burning than wood.

BEGINNING IN YUMA, ARIZONA

In writing this, I started to recollect my beginning. I was born in Yuma Arizona on December 26th, 1925. My first recollection of life that I remember was when I was four years old. Somehow or other, for the life of me I can't remember it came about, but I swallowed a penny. I remember my mother hitting me in the back just below the neck. Then trying to stick her fingers down my throat in order to get that damn penny out! The penny got stuck in my Adam's Apple for an instant and I felt fine, but my mother was in such a panic that she didn't give me time to explain that the penny was already settled in my stomach. The next thing she did was give me Olive Oil. I guess she thought the slick oil would make me get rid of the penny by sliding it out of me when I went to the bathroom. Even though I felt fine, she took me to the Doctor! There was nothing he could do except he told her to make me go to the bathroom in a pan, so she could sift through the solids, in order to find the penny. The next morning, she did just as the doctor had told her. Sure enough, there was that darn old penny. My mother called, "Chris, come here." I went to her and she took me over her lap and spanked the hell out of me! I mean, she hit my fanny really hard with her open hand! "That's for scaring me half to death and so that you will remember to never put anything in your mouth except food from now on." She then hugged me for the longest time and cried at the same time. This all happened in Yuma.

BEGINNINGS IN BISBEE, ARIZONA

The following year we moved to Bisbee. My Grandfather and Grandmother owned a big building and several houses on Chihuahua Hill. This group of buildings was known as "The Dabovich Block." The big building had a bar and barber shop downstairs and wooden steps alongside the inside of the building to the upstairs portion. There was a big, big dance hall with a fine hardwood floor. According to my dad, that building was a lively place where big dances were held there, years ago. The building stood empty. A reminder of what once was filled with gaiety and laughter.

We moved into one of the vacant houses that year. My sister and I didn't go to school until the following year rolled around. We were put into first grade at Central School. I could communicate in each of the languages I knew, but I was really shy. Both my sister and I adapted well. Pretty soon we felt good about school. Our classmates had accepted us and we were happy.

My Mother, normally a very strong woman, got sick with an infected breast. Because of my mothers' illness, my sister had to stay home to be with her throughout most of the school year. As a result, my sister was detained one more year in fourth grade while I was promoted to fifth. We both went on to finish High School, however, I was always one year ahead of her due to my mother's illness.

An incident occurred in school when I was in fourth grade. I went to school with a stomachache one day. Around ten o'clock in the morning, I got the urge to go to the bathroom. We had a very mean teacher by the name of Miss Hammator. We could not go to the pencil sharpener unless she checked the point on our pencils. I raised my hand and the teacher asked, "What is it?" I said, "May I go to the bathroom?", She responded, "Put your hand down and do your lesson." Well, I just had to go. I finally did. I felt myself being lifted from my chair, but I felt good! I was embarrassed because the rest of the class started to squirm and they were looking toward me. "Chris: !, Shouted Miss Hammator, "Is that you that went to the bathroom in class?" "Yes ma'am." I said, "I asked for permission and you did not grant it and I just couldn't hold it any longer." "Just get yourself off of your seat and go home and change" she said. I went home and Mother helped me bathe and put some other clothes on. I went back to school amid the stares and grins of the boys and girls in my class. The windows, which were normally closed were now wide open! The smell was gone. Miss Hammator got everybody's attention and made this announcement. "From now on, if anybody wants to g to the bathroom, just raise your hand." Needless to say I broke precedent, because the rest of the year, kids were going to and coming from the bathroom. I will venture to say that three fourths of those trips were unnecessary, but hey, she brought it on for not letting me go when I really needed to.

The year I started school, there was no such class as kindergarten. The grades were from first to fifth. School at Central went quite rapidly. Before I knew it, I was going to Horace Mann School on Quality Hill, These were grades sixth through eighth. There were so many kids to each grade that each grade had a number, for instance there were; 6-1, 6-2, 6-3, then from there 7-1, 7-2, 7-3 and 8-1, 8-2, 8-3. The more advanced students were in the 6-1, 7-1, 8-1. The three years in Horace Mann School were the dullest of all the years I spent in any school. My dad did not allow me to go out for sports and what he said, he meant.

Going to High School in Bisbee was the most gratifying times for me. Even now, I think of all the good time I had there.

I was coaching a Babe Ruth baseball team several years ago, when this boy, on our team said he wasn't coming to practice the next day because he was going to commencement exercises. He was going to graduate from the eighth grade to high school. I liked this boy a lot, so, I bought him a card and wrote, "Andy, the next four years of your life are going to be you're most enjoyable." I saw him about four years later and he said to me, "Mr. Dabovich, when I read what you wrote on that card four years ago, I just thought that they were just a bunch of words. But after I finished high school, I want to tell you that you were right. The four years at Bisbee High School were the memories of my life.

My dad had gone to a military school in New Mexico when he was very young. He played in a military band. Well, my first year in high school, as a freshman, my dad decided I should be in the high school band. I knew nothing about music, other than listening to it on the radio. My dad wet to school to talk with the band director. Next thing I knew, I was in the band! The director gave me a dented, silver sliding trombone to play. No case for it, just the ugly silver, dented trombone. The other students in the trombone section had their own instruments, cases and all. Beside, their trombones were nice and golden. I remember my first day with the band. I sat next to a senior girl by the name of Lois Gorden. She could really play her instrument. Man, the notes just poured out of her trombone loud and with authority. She looked at me and my pathetic trombone and said, "Let me see it a minute." I let her have it. She had difficulty moving the slide. She reached into her instrument case and took out a small bottle of oil for the slide. She worked the slide back and forth 'til the slide moved with ease. Then she handed it back to me. I learned how to read music, eventually. Lois brought some silver polish. Between the two of us, mostly Lois, we got the luster back to my trombone. The dents were still there, but the old trombone was shiny and the slide worked. I felt like I was really a member of the band now! I played in the band for three years, until I asked my mom if I could try out for the football team. She was reluctant at first, but she said Okay, and that made me feel really good.

I must tell of this incident when I was a freshman. In mid December, the band director told the band to be at the Court House on a particular Saturday. We were to escort Santa Clause into town to visit with the little children, so they could tell him what they wanted for Christmas. Well, it snowed the previous night. All night long! We didn't own a radio. We had no way of knowing if there was going to be a parade or not. We had no telephone either! Television was unheard of in 1944, in our house anyway. I put on my gray colored pants with a red stripe down the sides. My band jacked with was tomato red, with golden colored buttons the size of quarters, and a policeman type hat. I started walking up the street, about a mile to the Court House. Everything looked bright! The air was cool, but nice. There was no traffic, no people. As I'm trudging along toward the Court House I'm wondering, "Maybe the darn thing has been postponed and everybody but me knows about it." I finally got there. Nobody was around. The parade was to start in forty-five minutes. I waited for what seemed to me an eternity, then decided that there was not going to be a parade. I started walking toward home, when all of a sudden, I slipped and fell. As I fell, I did the splits. I got up quickly, looked around sheepishly, embarrassed that someone had seen me fall. But no, no one saw me. My pants had ripped open from the front to the back. I had to walk through Main Street to get home. I started walking and I felt like a cowboy wearing chaps! I knew that people would look at me because I had my band uniform on. It sticks out like a sore thumb in the contrasting snow. I decided to put everything out of my mind. I walked proudly past Main Street to my home. The following Saturday, the parade took place. By that time the snow had melted, my pants were repaired and an embarrassing incident forgotten.

When we were young, our parents didn't let us go anywhere. We just hung around home. When I joined the band, I saw my first football game. Boy! Was I surprised?! The football team had uniforms and helmets. In my mind, I pictured the football team playing in Levis and tee shirts and no helmets. I was in awe of my first football experience. We played our school songs and various others, then at half time, we went out on the field to perform. I'll never forget the first football game I ever attended, for as long as I live.

I concentrated on studies my first three years in high school. I was just an average student, content to get a passing grade, (which I did), and was just trying to get along. I never made the honor roll, never took "home work," home with me...never! The twelve years that I went to school, I was never late for class and best of all, I had perfect attendance for all twelve years!

In September 1944, I started my senior year. I was seventeen years old, but in three months I would turn eighteen. I wanted to play football because in my previous three years all I did was study, study, study. I went out for the team. Coach Waldo Dicus put me in left tackle. We only had about twenty-nine players. In hose days, a player played offense and defense. Practice days during the week were hectic for me. Not because of football practice, but because I didn't have a ride to the ball field. You see, the high school was in old Bisbee and the ball park where we practiced was in Warren, four miles away. My parents didn't have a car, so I would have to hitchhike to the Warren Ball Park every day for practice. One time a man on a motorcycle stopped and gave me a ride to the park. I had never been on a motorcycle before, and needless to say, I was a nervous wreck when I got to practice. I haven't been on another motorcycle since. Mostly people in cars would pick us up since some of us did not have cars ourselves. The players from Warren had their own cars or their parent's cars. No problem for them.

Our football schedule my senior year, had such schools as Tucson Amphi Theater, Douglas, Tombstone and Nogales. Tucson High School and St. Mary's of Phoenix were the power houses in those days. Tucson High School was on our schedule the very first game. I'm sure that Tucson regarded us as a tuneup because they played high schools from Phoenix, Tucson and Yuma. Bisbee High school was small school compared to theirs. Anyway, the Tucson Badgers got the scare of their lives when little old Bisbee High School went to play them.

The trip to Tucson was the very first for me. I was in awe of everything I saw. Big buildings, cars all over the place and fancy signs. I saw the stadium with about ten thousand people in the stands, the neat playing area where we were to play football, my God!! The grass was healthy green and neatly mowed. The yardage lines perfectly straight and about four inches wide. The night was cool and smelled of recently cut grass. Tucson High School had about the best football team assembled on the field hat September night. I was nervous as all get out. The game started and after I got blocked once and made my first tackle, my nervousness went away. The game itself was nip and tuck until late in the fourth quarter. The Tucson Badgers scored for the third time. The score ended up: Tucson 20 to Bisbee's 14. Even the Tucson fans applauded us after the gun ended the game.

In the locker room we were taking off our pads and uniforms, when dozens of what seemed to be dignitaries came in, shaking our hands, commenting on what a good game we played. We lost the game, but these guys were making us feel like we won the damn thing. Even the

Tucson Coach came in, stood at the big double wide door where he could be seen and said, "Nice game fellas," then he left. That was one of our two games we lost to Tucson High that year. Later on in the season they came down to our park and really beat up on us, 40 to 6. We won the rest of the games on or schedule that year though.

Nogales High School had a small, but scrappy team. Although we beat them in the scoring column, they beat us physically. They had a bunch of Mexican-Irish, Mexican-Indian and other half breeds that sure made our bodies sore. That Nogales Apache Team was the most hard hitting, physical team I had played against, of all the teams on our schedule! I won't outright say they were dirty players, but I for one, got my nuts twisted in a fumble recovery melee.

The first time I felt pain, I mean really bad pain, was when we played Tombstone High School at Warren Ball Park. It was maybe, the third game on our schedule. They Yellow Jackets had a fire plug looking running back, by the name of Oscar Gast. He was good! He was about five foot ten inches tall and weighed a good two hundred pounds. Other than Gast, the Tombstone team was mediocre at best. We were beating them pretty good that night. Gast was the whole offense for the Yellow Jackets. He ran the ball all the time for them. Late in the first half, Oscar came running over to my side of the line. I grabbed for him, caught his jersey as he went by me. All of a sudden he stopped dead in his tracks and reversed his field. I still had my fingers in his jersey and when he reversed his field to go back the other way he pulled my arm out of its socket. I still had my cleats planted in the sod and as my arm popped out, Gast went down. I felt like the end of the world had come. I was scared. I had never experienced pain such as I was having right then. Our Captain, Bill Penn came over and asked, "What's wrong Dabo"? . I told him, "I hurt my arm." Then we went up to the line of scrimmage and I hit this one guy with my hurt shoulder and my arm popped back in. I felt fine after that. We went on to win the game. After showering, I began to hitchhiked home. I got a ride from a family that had been to the game and knew me. When I got home, I went to bed. Around midnight, when my body had cooled down from the game, my arm begins to ache. I could not sleep that night. The following Monday, I went to Coach Waldo Dicus and told him about my arm. He took me to the Copper Queen Hospital in old Bisbee. We saw Dr. Rice. Now, Dr. Rice wore a hearing aid and was up there in age. He said to me, "Pop your arm." I said, "your crazy Doc, I can't pop it." It hurts too much when it's out of place anyway. He then examined me and told me that my ligaments were probably torn. He told me that if I got operated on, to repair the torn ligaments, that I would probably have to go to the Mayo Clinic in Minnesota. My dad was working for W.P. A. at the time, getting about $33.00 a month plus commodities. We had no insurance and the Doctor says for me to go to Minnesota to have my shoulder repaired, I'm afraid not. Needless to say, I didn't go. My arm, to this day, is still the same as when I hurt it. I have to sleep on my stomach with my right arm under me, for fear that it might "pop out," in my sleep. The pain is unexplainable. It's very intense. I would not wish this pain on anyone, not even my worst enemy.

If I may digress, I would like to tell about the time I was twelve. I always wanted to be a Boy Scout. All my friends belonged to a Boy Scout troop, all except for me. I wanted to be a Scout, not for the reason for other boys were scouts....but because I like the Boy Scout hat! I asked my mother if I could join. To my amazement she said, "Yes." We didn't have too much money in those days. To my parents a Boy Scout uniform was a luxury. So, I told them I was going to buy my uniform little by little. I went to my first meeting. The Scout Master told me I had to buy a Boy Scout Manual. I told him I would try to have one for the next meeting. That week, I sold gunny sacks, pop bottles, etc. Saved every penny I could get my hands on. I eventually bought a Scout Manual. Slowly, I started to buy the rest of the uniform. First, I bought the neckerchief with the scout ring to hold the ends together. It took me a long, long time to save enough to buy my leggings, my shirt and my pants. I eventually bought all of it. I had everything, except what I joined the Scouts for...the hat. That item turned out to be the most expensive. I guess my mother felt sorry for me at this point, because she gave me the money to buy the hat. Man, oh man! Was I in seventh heaven with that hat! I wore it all the time! I don't know if I looked good in it or not, but I had it and that was all that mattered to me! I kept going to the Boy Scout meetings. Not that I was interested in the discussions, but for the games we played afterwards. I especially liked the game, "Hounds and Hares." A group of boys would go out in the street, with some chalk, and mark the street with the arrow -----> in the direction that they were going. They would mark this every 30 or 50 feet or so and keep on going. They were the HARES. Then about ten minutes later, (The Hounds) would go outside to look for the first markings of an arrow, then the second and so on 'til the Hares were caught. Sometimes the Hares would double back to the Scout Hall and wait for the Hounds to return. To me, it was such a fun game! I studied my hand book. I made my first step as a Scout. I made, "Tenderfoot." As a twelve-year old, I put my Scout uniform on the fourth of July. Our Scout Master told us to be in town, ready to help people to cross the street, you know, little things like that. Well, I didn't help anybody cross the street that day. I just went walking among the crowd in my new uniform, and of course, my brand-new hat! I had a wonderful time doing absolutely nothing. Oh, Yes, there was one incident that happened on the fourth of July that year. Some friends of mine had fire crackers and they gave me a few. I would light them and When the fuse got really short, I would throw them up in the air where they would pop. I was doing all right until I got one fire cracker which had a short fuse to start with. I lit the fuse, cocked my arm to throw it and it exploded in my hand. I felt a burning sensation on one side of my fingers. When I looked at my hand, my index finger had split open! Ouch! It looked like a wiener looks after it's been boiled in water. I took my neckerchief from around my neck, wrapped it around my finger and hand, stuck my hurt hand in my pocket and went home. My parents never found out about the incident. It was about two weeks before my finger finally healed. I had to quit the Boy Scouts because my dad said that all the scout activities were keeping me from my duties at home. I quit the Scouts, but I cherished my Boy Scout hat for years to come.

After a football season was over in my senior year at school, I decided to try out for the basketball team. I got to be very good at dribbling, shooting and rebounding in Physical Education class, so I thought I would give it a try. I made the team. Only ten guys went out for the team. All of us were on the football team, with the exception of Benny Dominguez. We thought that we were in shape to go from football to basketball. Wrong! We had to retrain our bodies to play basketball.

We played a total of twenty-six games that year, including Conference and State Tournament games. We ended our season with an eighteen win and eight loss record. We went to Phoenix to play in the State Tournament. We were immediately eliminated by Glendale High School. Tucson High School beat North Phoenix High School in the tourney. In those days, schools weren't classified as 5A, 4A, 2A, A, B or C. The schools with the best records played each other. If you drew a big school, tough!

I would like to digress once again, if I may.

Living on Chihuahua Hill wasn't so bad when I was a kid. There was a vacant lot next to our house, approximately one hundred fifty feel long by "Mountain Wide." By that I mean, the lot was on the sloping side of the mountain. That's where we played football. Our football was an empty Carnation Milk can. My mother would save the cans for me. I would take the wrapping off the can and there was my football. I was thirteen. Since I was the oldest of the kids who played, I made myself the passing quarterback. One of my neighbors, Mert Mendez and my younger sister, Christina played, as well as other kids whose names I can't recall. Mert gave Christina the name, "Gilda." The field like I pointed out, was on a slope. There were big boulders there, bed springs, weeds, small stinky trees and more weeds and lots of rocks. Every play we had, I would have Christina, my little sister run up hill toward a big boulder, then cut straight across. The ball (milk can) would be there. Christina had a great pair of hands and was a fast runner. She turned out to be a great receiver on this Chihuahua Hill "playing field." We played football every day and enjoyed it. I threw that can so much that I was actually spiraling that sucker and the kids were catching it. We would quit when our "football," would get so dented it wouldn't carry any distance. Surprisingly and fortunately, one got hurt. No broken bones or sprained ankles. Sure there were small cuts, bruises and little scrapes, but we didn't care. We were having fun that ignored all the hurts. Ah, memories.

When I was about fourteen, maybe fifteen around there, I played a lot of baseball and a lot of fast pitch softball. A softball is harder to hit than a baseball, believe it or not. Here is the reason why. In baseball, the pitching mound is sixty feet, six inches from home plate. In fast pitch softball, the pitching rubber is forty feet to the plate. So, in baseball when you swing at the pitched ball, you have time to unlock your hips and swing at th pitch. In softball, you don't have that luxury. You have to swing immediately when that ball is on top of you, because you take a baseball "cut" at the softball, the catcher is already throwing the ball back to the pitcher. So that is the difference.

On a particular Sunday, the fast pitch team on which I played, scheduled a game with some soldiers from Fort Huachuca. The game began innocently enough. Then a G.I. got on base. I was playing first base. A ground ball was hit to shortstop. He threw to second base to force the runner out when the second baseman and the runner collided at the bag. The umpire called the runner out on the force play, but our second baseman lay writhing in pain. I called "time," ran to him and asked," what's the matter, Wimpy?" He said, "That son of-a-bitch spiked me.". We looked at the soldier's shoes. He was wearing green army sneakers. I said, "Wimpy, he couldn't have spiked you, the poor guy is wearing tennis shoes." Wimpy replied, "I don't care what he is wearing, it still hurts."

Another time I went to Horace Mann Field, where all softball games were played. On the pitching mound was a very colorful player by the name of Paul Pavlovich. He had been wounded in te war. He had lost an eye and his face was a little bit disfigured. People didn't see him as a handicapped person at all. The game started. He was pitching a good game for a couple of innings. Around the third or fourth inning, Paul pitched the ball, then he hollered, "Time," fell to his knees sifting through the dirt, looking for something. When he found what he was looking for, Paul turned toward Center Field and put both his hands on his face. What happened was this; when Paul pitched that last pitch, his glass eye popped out of his eye socket. He called time out, dropped to his knees, found the eye, cleaned it on his pants, turned to Center Field and put the eye back in. He continued to pitch. Incidently, he won the game. I though that was the most bizarre thing I had ever witnessed up to this point.

Another time, this ball player by the name of Glen O'Leary, (what a magnificent ball player he was. Smooth, graceful and happy go lucky), hit a tremendous drive way out into the deepest part of right field. As the right fielder ran after the ball, Glen dropped his bat and he went down to the ground at home plate. He had lost his false teeth as he swung at the ball. He picked up his teeth, rubbed them on his thigh, put them in his mouth and ran to first base. In the meantime, the right fielder had thrown the ball back to the second baseman, who threw to first base. Glen was out on a bang, bang play. People were laughing. Glen, the good sport that he was, came back to his dugout, took off his cap and bowed to the fans in attendance.

I played a lot on Horace Mann Field. We were playing a very good team, which had a black player whose name was Nate Hickman. The young man was about twenty to twenty-two years of age. He had a very violent temper. The game began. Things were going quite nicely, until Nate came to bat. The umpire on this particular night was Angel Salas, In his day, Angel was quite an athlete in his own right. Angel was good in football, basketballs, horseshoes, playing cards, golf, you name it, he was above average in all of them. Even bowling. He had a younger brother, Charlie. He loved to ride horses. He told me one day, "I don't envy my brother, because he is good at any sport he chooses, but he is not as good as me at riding horses." Anyway, back to the game at hand. Hickman gets comfortable in the batter's box and Hickman hits a long drive toward left field, ...foul... strike one! The second pitch comes in, he fouls this one as well, ...strike two! Nate anchors his feet in the dirt. Here comes the pitch. The umpire yells, "Strike." Hickman is out. He stands there for about five seconds, then, he throws his bat about thirty feet up in the air. The umpire Mr. Salas, whips off his mask, goes over to Hickman and says, "Young man, if that bat comes down, you are out of the game." Needless to say, Hickman spent the rest of the game on the bench. Hickman's team eventually won the game. I suppose he went home happy.

If Horace Mann Field could talk, it would have some doozies of stories to tell. The very first time that I played an organized game, was on Horace Mann Field. I can remember as if it were yesterday I was fourteen years of age, five feet eleven inches in height and weighed about 160 pounds. My parents had given me permission to go watch a softball game at Horace Mann Field. The Elks Lodge had a pretty good team. They were playing some other team for first place. Both teams were warming up when the manager of the Elks team comes over to the bleachers where I was sitting and asked me, "Hey kid, you want to play? We are a man short." Excitedly, I responded, "Heck yeah!" When

I got to their bench, I told the manager, Beryl Dunkerson, "I don't have a glove, and I'm left-handed." He responded, "Don't worry about a mitt, we'll get you one." He did.

Dunkerson got his team together, reminding them that they were playing for first place. He told them if they made an error to, "Shake it off," forget it and keep on playing. Then he turned to me and said, "Dabovich, you go to right." We were the home team, so we went out to our positions in the field. The game was scoreless until the third inning. There was a man on first, a man on second, with one out. The following batter hit the ball to me in right field. I caught the ball for the second out. The runner on second tagged and ran to third. I threw the ball to third base, but the third baseman couldn't catch it. It was about thirty feet over his head. In fact, the ball landed out in the street! Both runners scored. Above all the shouting and noise, I could hear the manager, who also played second base say, "Come on, Candy Arm!" The next batter hit a medium fly ball to me, in right field. Finally the inning was over. I came to the dugout. Everybody was quiet, except the manager, who said, "Forget about it Candy Arm." The Elks scored two runs on their half of the inning. It remained two to two until the last half of the seventh inning. In softball, seven innings are regulation. Well, wouldn't you know it. The first batter in our last inning was me. Again, the manager yells, "Come on Candy Arm, get something started!" Here I was, fourteen years of age, never played in a league game in my life and the manger is urging me on like I was a franchise player. The first pitch came in. I swung from the heels and missed. Strike one! I felt awful! I said to myself, "I'll probably get it again from that son-of-a-bitch if I strike out." Good thing that I'm the first batter, because somebody can make the last out, not me. That's some consolation. I got back in the batter's box. Here comes the next pitch. My God, I couldn't believe it, the ball was right there in the middle of the plate, begging to be hit. I swung and saw the ball rise up into the night on its way to right field, as I ran to first base. It felt great! I got a lump in my throat as I saw the right fielder just stand there as the ball sailed about fifty feet over his head. I rounded the bases. All the Elks players were waiting for me at home plate. They all patted me on the back. Even the manager, who remarked "I knew you were good for something Candy Arm. Nice going!" I couldn't sleep that night I could not believe that I had won a game for the team. It was great!!! Just great!!! That game propelled me to lots of years of organized baseball, softball, basketball and all other sports in my life.

At this point in my story, you might think, what does all this sports talk have to do with Chihuahua Hill? Well, I lived there while I was doing all these things. Now, I"ll have more to say about my neighborhood.

One of our neighbors, the Mendez family, lived up from us, across the steps, kitty corner from our house. They were a nice family. The husband and father of the kids was named Mike. He liked to drink a lot. I'm not criticizing him. Just saying he liked to drink. He also liked to play his washboard. He would put thimbles on his fingers and "strum" the washboard while listening to music and singing along with the radio. To tell you the truth, it sounded quite good! Mr. Mendez was killed in a motorcycle accident at a young age. In those days' families used to have the body and wakes at their homes. The neighbors were gathered at the Mendez home mourning Mr. Mendez, when his brother, Raphael came into the room where the body laid in the coffin. He approached the coffin, he reached in and sat his dead brother up in the coffin. People started running out of the house screaming.

Mike Jr., the eldest of the Mendez children, had real long legs when he was young. He used to leave his house by running down the concrete steps, three or four at a time. He never fell. I don't know of anyone else that could do that. I bet, that if they made running down some flight of steps an Olympic event, Mike would have come home with the Gold Medal.

Mike had two sisters, Delia and Irma. He also had a brother, Mert who played on our "ball field." Their mother, Anita, was a very nice lady. She always called me Crisito. My family liked them a lot.

The Castellano family lived directly above and in back of us. They were a large family. By large, I mean there were a lot of them. There was the mother, Simona, her husband, Evaristo and daughters, Candelaria, Panchita, Inez, Vicka and Juan (female). The sons were Rafael, Sixto, Policarpio, Angel and Guadalupe. To this day we call Guadalupe, "Choyleh." I don't know why. The daughters were older than me and my sister Florence. They would call us to their house, once in a while and put on variety acts for us. It was a lot of fun! We liked that very much. I saw Angel and Sixto play softball at Horace Mann Field. They were good ball players. Both of them!

Behind them lived Carmen Miranda and her family. I guess her husband was dead because I never knew him. Mrs. Miranda had a son named Chato. He came to my house and borrowed my glove because he was going to try out for the local professional baseball I never saw my glove again. That was okay, though, because I had another one. A first baseman's trap mitt. The one I loaned him was a five-finger baseball glove. By that time I was playing a lot of amateur baseball as a first baseman. It was March 1950. I was twenty-two years old. That was when I almost became a pro!

I was bowling on a team at the Warren Bowling Lanes on a Monday night. I noticed that every time I bowled a ball down the alley, when I turned to come back to sit down, I would see this bald headed man just kept his eyes on me. It made me feel very uneasy. It got so bad that every time I rolled the ball down the alley. I would return to my seat with my head lowered.

After the bowling match, I changed shoes and was about to leave when Glen O'Leary came over to me and said, "Chris, there is someone ere I'd like you to meet." "Okay," I replied, as he led me to the bald headed man, who was still sitting in the same chair. "Chris, this is Sid Cohen, manager of the Bisbee-Douglas Baseball Club," said Glen. I immediately recognized him as I extended my hand and shook his. Mr. Cohen said, "I understand you play baseball. Mr. O'Leary tells me that you play first base." I said, "Yes." He then continued, "I need a first baseman on my club and wondered if you would like to try out for the team." I asked, "Don't you have already have Manny Magallon?" He replied, "He doesn't want to sign his contract. We have exhausted all our efforts to sign him." I said, "Okay, but I have a job already." He acted like he didn't hear me.

The next practice day was going to be on a Saturday. Mr. Cohen asked, "Can you be at the Warren Ball Park on Saturday morning? Just bring your glove and shoes. We'll furnish you with the rest." I answered, "All right, I'll be there at eight." Saturday morning I rode the local bus to Warren Ball Park. There were some guys there already. Pretty soon their team bus came with Sid Cohen driving it. He said, "Good morning." So did I. He then told me that he forgot to tell me that the team was going to practice in Douglas at the Copper King Stadium. I said that was all right since I didn't have anything else to do.

When we got there, they gave me sanitary socks, jock strap, stirrups, cap and the uniform, which fortunately fit me just right. We went out to the field to warm up. I had seen some of the players from the previous year, so that put me at ease. Pretty soon, after warming up, Cohen told me to go to first base, after telling the fellows that my name was Chris. Cohen went up into the stands, where some Douglas businessmen were. We started infield practice. Since I played amateur baseball, infield practice was no big deal with me. At this point I didn't feel any pressure. I kept looking up at the grandstand. I'm sure he was evaluating me. We worked on infield drills for almost an hour, then he came down on the field and told us to come to the dugout. We had batting practice for about two hours. The team had two decent pitchers who were from Mexico. They pitched batting practice. Again, Mr. Cohen returned to the grandstand to watch batting practice. I struck up a conversation with both of the Mexican pitchers, namely "Blackie" Morales and "Chato" Belol. When it came to my turn at bat, they would holler at me "Curva," or "Recta," which meant curve or fastball, what they were going to throw to me. I hit several baseballs over the fence in right field and a lot of "ropes" to right and right center. Those two pitchers were all right by me. Sid Cohen came down from the from the stands and said, "Lets take one quick turn at infield practice, then go take a shower." By then it was noon.

I showered, put on my clothes, folded the uniform and took it to his office. He said, "Kid you looked good out there. You're built just right for baseball. I"m impressed. Here's the deal; I"ll give you $225.00 a month for your services." I replied, "I'm afraid I can't accept that amount. I'm making fifty dollars more at my present job and I'm barely making it." "But you are single," he responded. I said, "Yes, I am, but I'm supporting my mother, two sisters, two brothers and myself, and I"m barely making it with $275.00. He said, "Sorry kid, that's all I can offer you. Too bad for both of us. Oh by the way, the team has been invited to dinner today at 6:00 p.m., your welcome to come." I said, "Thanks for the tryout and the dinner offer, but I have to get home." We shook hands and I started walking from the Douglas Stadium to Bisbee. It took me forever, just to get to the outskirts of town. Since I didn't have any money, I walked and walked and walked. At the underpass, on the outskirts of Douglas a car stopped and gave me a ride all the way to my house. It was a Bisbee family that had been visiting relatives in Douglas. I didn't know who they were, but they recognized me. It was about 3:00 p.m. when I got home, starving and tired. I was glad to be home! So, as you see, I almost became a "pro." Oh well, those were nice memories. I just continued playing amateur spots for a long time, still living in the same old house on Chihuahua Hill.

A lot of responsibility lay on my shoulders when my father died. My mother was strictly a housewife. She wasn't about to get a job anywhere. I wouldn't have permitted it anyway.

Phelps Dodge was going into mining on Chihuahua Hill. Our house was built on their property. We had acquired some lots on Naco Highway, so we had a house built on one of the lots in 1956. We moved that year. Soon after, Phelps Dodge Corporation started blasting on Chihuahua Hill. Chihuahua Hill is now part of the Lavender Pit.

The families that lived on Chihuahua Hill are scattered all throughout the community. Some of the older folks have died, including my dear mother, but the younger generation is still around, although much older, I'm sure they still remember the warmth and friendship we all had on Chihuahua Hill.

Going back a bit, I must tell how every Saturday morning my mother would line us up in the kitchen and give us a tablespoon of Caster Oil. "Yuk"!! We weren't even sick either. But it was a ritual, every darn Saturday we had Caster Oil! My younger brother, John was skinny as a young boy. Not only did he get Caster Oil, he also got a big, large tablespoonful of Cod Liver Oil. We all hated it. But by God, we all grew up healthy, not sickly. I thank my mother for that now, even though at the time, I thought it was cruel for us to have to take that thick Caster Oil. My poor brother, John. My mother was so worried because he was so skinny that she took him to the doctor and he put him on a "reverse" diet. Sure enough, he started gaining weight.

Speaking of John. I remember one day a lady came to our house. She asked Mom if she could "borrow" John for a few minutes. Well, what the lady didn't know was that none of us ever went anywhere, except to school, without Mom. Of course, my mother said, "No, he can't go." The lady told my mother that she could go with John to her house and explained to her why. It seems that this lady had a little girl about five years old that had the hiccups steady for about a month. The lady found out that one of my mother's children was named John, and she had been told that a person named John had healing powers. My mother, a devout Catholic, didn't believe in such "nonsense," so she said, "Yes I'll go to your house with my son." I asked if I could go and she said, "Yes," so we all went. We got to the lady's house. My mother asked the lady, "Just what do you want my son to do?" The lady said, "All he has to do is touch my little girl." I could see the little girl sitting on a chair at their dinning table. John, at the time was about nine years old. He didn't know why he was there. My mom told him to just go over and put his hand on the little girl's shoulder. John resisted. He didn't want to be there in the first place. He didn't know what he was doing there. The lady was very hospitable. She gave my mother some hot coffee and some cookies for all of us. After a while, my mother told John, "The sooner you put your hand on her shoulder, the sooner we can all go home." John sprang up from his chair, went over to the little girl, put his hand on her shoulder and went over to mother and said, "O.K. Mom, let's go home now." The lady hugged John, thanked my mother and we all came home. A couple of days later, my mother saw the lady and asked her if her daughter's hiccups had quit. The lady said yes, about a half hour after we left her house. Another time, another lady came by and wanted a piece of cloth from John's clothes. My mother cut a small piece off John's undershirt and gave it to the lady. She was going to put the piece of cloth on one of her kids, so the child would get well. We never found out what happened. That ended my brother, John's healing powers because we were never asked again. John never knew he had such "powers," because my mother never explained it to him. Shades of Oral Roberts. Now that I am an adult, I have found out that there are such people who have the power to heal and they don't know it. But, their names have to be----John!

Chihuahua Hill was so rocky that nothing grew there but weeds. The gas and water lines had to be laid on top of the ground because it was impossible to bury the pipes. In the winter, when the temperature would get below freezing, the water pipe lines would freeze. When that happened, the following morning when the sun would shine, there would be bursted lines. If these pipes didn't get repaired quickly, at night fall the water would freeze. The next morning the whole mountain side would look like an ice castle, a very lovely spectacle!

The houses on Chihuahua Hill had to be level of course. In order to do this, a rock front would first be built, then fill thrown behind these walls of rock. Then you could figure on building a house on the face of this Chihuahua Hill mountain. When Phelps Dodge tore down the houses, all that remained were the sturdy rock walls. The foundations could be seen where houses once stood on top of them. Th houses were solidly built: I know what when the wind blew, you could not feel it inside. When it rained, the houses didn't leak.

When I was a child, my mother took us to visit someone. In their house, I saw a big old piano. I cannot imagine, for the life of me, how they ever got that whale of a piano up on the mountain and into the house!

Although, the houses looked kind of rustic, some were really nice. The inside of these houses were very clean and orderly. No one ever locked their doors when they would go out any where. Everyone trusted everyone else. Therefore, there was no need to lock the homes. I don't think we even owned a key our house. Some of the houses had nice yards. No grass yards, just yards with patches of flowers, very pretty, colorful flowers. Some homeowners had their little gardens where they grew tomatoes, chili, squash and other vegetables. Most of these gardens would grow in half barrows or boxes filled with soil brought in from somewhere else. The families living on Chihuahua Hill were some of the most motivated people in Bisbee. They made plants and flowers bloom in the hardest of conditions. They took pride in their work and finished products.

My mother would take us to visit different neighbors that she knew. All of them would eventually show my mom their flower or vegetable gardens. There would be an air of pride as the ladies, or sometimes the man of the house would talk about how they babied their vegetables and flowers.

There was a black burro who wondered around the Hill. It belonged to a man who lived alone in a small house adjacent to a small shack. We all knew that the burro's name was "La Chanata." What the name signified, I hadn't the slightest idea. When I inquired about the name, a person told me that possibly it was named after the"Chanate" bird, who was also black. "La Chanata," was accepted by everyone. She was treated with tenderness. She would spend her days grazing along th face of the mountain. At night, she would be in the little shack Don Manuelitio had for her. The houses took on a different look at night. Some of the houses were built very long. Maybe one hundred feet long. Looking up Chihuahua Hill from the road at night, these long houses would look like passenger cars on a train. A marvelous sight indeed!

At one time or another, these people would attend Mass on Sundays, since all he people on the Hill were of the Catholic faith. My neighbors would walk down the steps, alongside our house, dressed in nice clothes going to church. Our family, with the exception of my dad, would also go to church on Sundays and other religious days. As a matter of fact, when I was eight to twelve years old, I served as an Altar Boy. My mother "volunteered" me. I enjoyed being an Altar Boy. The only thing I didn't like was when the priest started with the incense. The smell would get to me every time and I'd get nauseated.

Some of my duties as an Altar Boy were to light the candles, whether for Mass or Rosary, then snuff them out, with the snuffer, after the services. Also, change the Missile from on side of the altar to the other. Why? I never asked. During the collection, I liked going up the aisles passing the collection plate. I got to see people, especially the girls that came to church. Another reason I liked going up the aisles was that it gave me a chance to stretch my legs, since we were always kneeling at the altar.

During Lent, people seemed more subdued. The statues and portraits were covered with dark cloth. It remained that way for the forty days of Lent. I liked Lent and never tired of listening to the priest talk about when Jesus was crucified, the days leading up to it and what happened after the Crucifiction. Then following Good Friday, on Holy Saturday, there was a joyous Mass with lots of music and singing. The Altar was adorned with flowers of all kinds. The drab, dark cloths came off the statues and portraits. It was truly a special and joyous occasion. Jesus had risen! Participating at those Masses would give me goose bumps!

At Christmas, whoever was in charge would decorate one corner of the front Altar with the nativity scene. It would be done in large scale; branches would be cut and brought in from the hill. Hay and all the other trimmings, that make up a manger, were added. The figures were the biggest ones I had ever seen. When the scene was finished, all we wanted to do was to be there, admiring it, for long periods of time. It was quite an attraction! Someone got the idea of putting a plate or bowl at the scene. People would put nickels, dimes, quarters, fifty cent coins and dollar bills in the plate or bowl. I never knew who took the money or what it was used for.

At home, Christmas was always festive. My sister, Florence, with my help, would decorate the "live" Christmas tree. During Christmas Week, especially my mother, would cook different meals, bake cookies and make candy. My mother was good at everything that she attempted to do. If one of us in the family got sick, she had the right home remedy to make us well. Nothing rattled her. She was an excellent carpenter. If a screen was torn on a door or window, she would repair them. If there ever was a leak on the roof of the house, she would go up to the roof and fix that. She liked working outdoors, like cleaning the yard. She would take the initiative and we would follow her lead getting the job done. My mother was a born leader. She was very correct. She had a good sense of humor, however, she didn't let herself get too much into nonsense. I could always tell when she was in a bad mood, which wasn't too often.

The only vice Mom had was Bingo. Bingo was played every evening at different places like: Sacred Heart Church Hall, Serbian Church Hall, Elks Lodge, VFW, American Legion Post Hall and so on. She wet to Bingo six times a week! My Dad used to call her the "Tin Horn Gambler." She always came home with winnings. You might ask, "What is so great about that?" Well, the "great" part was that she only played ONE card all night long I asked her once, "Mom, why don't you play two or more cards, then your chances of winning are greater?" She replied, "You only win with ONE card."

She would walk to the Bingo parties. She never hitchhiked, however, if a car stopped for her and she knew who they were, she would get in. Getting home was no problem. There was always someone going her way, to drive her home.

My Dad was a big man physically. He liked to wear bib overalls. He always wore BVD'S', winter or summer. He is the only man that I know of, that never wore shorts. He was a very good worker. After work and supper my Dad would relax. He would go out on the porch to smoke an M & O cigar and down one pint of whiskey every evening. He never went to a bar to drink. He always drank at home. When my Dad wasn't working, he would go around our property picking up a piece of paper here or there. He was always picking up debris to make his property look clean. He was a stickler for cleanliness.

My Dad was a butcher by trade, however once in a while he worked for WPA and the utility company. Dad took pride n his work as a meat cutter. He had lots of customers. They all liked him because he treated them fairly. He knew his customers, as far as to what kind of meat cuts they wanted. At times, cut meat was put back in the show case for the next day sale. He would tell his customers not to pick on the meat that was in the show case. He would 'fresh cut' the meat for his preferred customers to whatever they wanted.

Dad told me that the meat that was left over, the owners of the butcher shop would sprinkle some kind of powder on the meat, rub it a little bit and color would come to the meat. It would look fresh cut, but in reality it was meat cut the previous day. He would sell this meat, however, not to "his" favorite customers.

Dad got me my first paying job at this store. I would help around the store, sweep the floor and help the clerks with the customers. On Saturday nights, my brother Ted and I would help clean the butcher blocks. Also, Ted would get inside the meat case to clean the glass from the inside. I would clean the glass from the outside. It was tiresome. After everything was clean, the owners would give Ted two dollars and I would get paid three dollars. The first job I ever had for pay was for three dollars a week. I'd go home really happy and give the three dollars to Mom. Three dollars was a fortune to me.

Our house was one of the last houses on Chihuahua Hill to get gas run to it. Dad worked part time for the Arizona Edison Company.

One day, after work, he and another worker put three-quarter inch pipe from outside, into our rooms, on top of the floor, along side the walls. We bought a couple of gas heaters, put one in our front room and one in our parent's room. Our rooms continued to be cold, however, we had lots of blankets to keep us warm, when we would go to bed. We continued to use wood in our kitchen stove. Since we didn't have a hot water heater, we would heat water on the stove, pour the water into a wash tub, that was placed on the kitchen floor for our night baths. Mom would help us with the baths. When my sister and Mom would bathe, the door was closed. When we were kids, that's just the way it was and we accepted it.

At the store that I was working in, at the age of ten, there was a man, in his late sixties. He was of slim build, wiry and could out drink a dozen men before he would pass out. This old gentleman's job was to kill chickens at the store to sell. I never knew his true given name. Everyone affectionately called him "Pancho Pelagallos". Since everyone called him by that name with sincerity, not to ridicule him, he accepted the name. In English, "Pancho Pella-gallos" means, "Frank the chicken plucker."

In the late thirty's, the mines were booming here in Bisbee, Arizona. The Miners Meat Market, where I worked, was where a lot of the miners would buy their groceries. They would buy and charge their groceries and pay up every two weeks, on their pay day. After settling up with te owners, the miners would go to the little back room with a few beers. This back room served as a warehouse, a garage to keep the delivery truck at night and also housed two chicken coops. While there the miners would drink their beer, relax, talk shop, then they would head home. They also shared a few beers with, "Pancho Pelagallos." Several times, I would see the poor old man stagger out of the store, weaving his way home.

I liked working with Pancho. He showed me how to kill the chickens and pluck them to get them ready for the customers. He would get a clucking chicken between his legs, get it by the head, stretch its neck and shove a sharp knife in a certain part of the neck. He would then throw the dying chicken into a 55-gallon drum. The chicken would shake and move around, making the most scraping noise in the metal drum, 'til it died. Next he would pick up the dead chicken out of the drum by its feet and dunk the chicken into another big metal drum, which had boiling water. He would dunk it four or five times, put it on a meat block that he had back there and proceed to pluck the feathers off the chicken 'till they were all gone. The smell of wet feathers in hot water made for an awful odor. After the chicken was plucked, Pancho would put the customer's name card on one of the chicken's legs. He would push a button, which made a ringing noise behind the counter at the store. The clerk would go back there, get the chicken and wrap it for the waiting customer. It was a very good business in those days. Nice fresh chickens to take home to cook any way the lady of the house chose, to prepare it as a meal.

It is comical to me now, how the ladies would choose the chickens they wanted when they went shopping. The man clerk would take the lady customer to the back, where the two big chicken coops were located. There were always about fifty chickens in each coop along with two nice and healthy looking red chickens. When the ladies would pick the chicken they liked, they would always pick the nice, big red one. The clerk would have Pancho go into the coop. The chickens would start to run every which way and squawk up a storm. Pancho would then get the big red that the customer wanted. She would touch its legs and body and say to the clerk, "This is the one I want." Then she would leave the area. The clerk would tell Pancho, "Throw the chicken back and kill another one." This Pancho did. That pretty big red chicken was always picked by the customer as the chicken they wanted, but they never knew the difference. Once they got home, they cooked the one that was already plucked. The red chicken lived in that coop for many months. Customers would always pick it as the chicken they wanted, but the chicken they wanted, but the chicken they took home was never the chicken they chose. Guess that is what is called, "Tricks of the trade." What you don't know won't hurt you.

To the West of Chihuahua Hill on Naco Road, live the Cota family. I got to be friends with Albert, the Cota's son, who was my age. He was very intelligent boy, well dressed and brought up right. We went to high school together and graduated the same year–1945. He always made the Honor Roll and I was glad for him. He never looked down on me because I wasn't as bright as he. I use to go to his house quite often. When I walked up to the porch, there was a big, wooden barrel which contained water. Just above the barrel was a faucet which dripped constantly. The faucet had been used for so many years that it was worn smooth. The outer part of the barrel had algae all around it. When we played ball at Albert's house and got thirsty, we would all run up to the barrel and drink water either from the faucet or from the barrel. Mrs. Cota had something that looked like a ladle, I guess it was a ladle, which we stuck under the faucet or dipped into the barrel. I usually drank the water out of the barrel because it was really cold water. You could look down into the barrel through the water and see the whole inside of the wooden barrel. I guess the, "seaweed," on the outside of the barrel, kept the water cool. The porch was old, but spacious. We would rest there after playing ball for a couple of hours. That house, like ours, was torn down for progress. The existing highway is there now. There are no signs of any rock wall foundation to look at as remembrance.

Coming home from High School one day, there on our porch sat my Mother with a three colored cat on her lap. I was very much surprised, because we never had pets of any kind, while growing up! I asked, "Where did you get the cat"? . Sofia Ruiz gave it to me, I liked the colors on it so, I accepted it," she replied. The cat was white, black and yellowish orange. She named the cat, Thumbolina. One day we heard the darndest noises in our small yard. I went outside to see what it was. I saw two dogs just rip that poor cat apart. They ran when they saw me. By that time my Mother had come out of the house to see what was the matter. I went up to our little yard to see Thumbolina, but she was all chewed up and dead. I looked up at my Mother. All she did was turn around and went inside the house. That cat had only lasted three days and was killed. We never got another animal, bird or pet since. My Mother got attached to that cat in jut three days. She soon forgot the incident and life went on as usual.

My Mother was tough, but also tender. My Mother was strongest when any one of us got sick. The food she gave us when we were ill, seemed to taste better then when we weren't sick. By sick, I mean; tonsillitis, measles, chicken pox, etc., that sort of thing which all kids get when they are young. A necessary evil, I suppose. She knew how to take care of us though.

After I graduated from High School, I went to several places looking for work. One place I went to was the Arizona Edison Company office, a few blocks from my house. Arizona Edison in Bisbee had the electric, water and gas departments. They also owned the bus system, the sewer system in the Warren area, and the Ice Plant in Lowell, a suburb of Bisbee. I talked to the man in charge. To my surprise he told me they needed help at the Ice Plant. Needless to say, that was my first job after graduation.

At home, after work one Saturday, I was sitting around for about an hour, when my brother Ted, two years my junior, came running in all excited! "Chris, there's a house on fire around the corner from here, let's go see!" I said. "Let's go!" Sure enough, as we went out, we could see the smoke rising to the sky, just west of our house on Chihuahua Hill. When we got there, we saw an old looking house, with black, putrid smelling smoke coming out of the windows of the burning house. The mountain side looked kind of colorful with people dotting it all around, watching. Firemen were just getting there when we arrived, pulling on a water hose. The Fire Chief by the name of Johnnie Hughes, was among the firemen. All of them were up in age. They had been firemen all their lives, I suppose, because when I use to go by City Hall where the fire truck was, I would see these men sitting on benches in front of the Fire House smoking they're, 'roll your own' cigarettes. There was hardly ever a fire in Bisbee. Whenever there was a fire, seems the whole town would converse on the scene and mill around out of curiosity. My brother Ted and I stood there watching the burning flames and smoke. As the firemen approached the flaming house, the Fire Chief yelled out, "Will a couple of fellows give us a hand?" No one moved to help, so Ted and I decided to help. We went over to the fire Chief and asked, "Just what do you want us to do?" He replied, "Grab the hose and get behind the firemen. They are going into the house to dowse the fire." Agreeing to this, we lined up behind the Chief and two old crusty firemen, grabbed the hose and went into the burning house. Someone turned the water on. The hose was about four inches in circumference, suddenly filled with water and got hard as a rock. We couldn't see a thing, for the room was pitch black with smoke. We heard the Chief say, "To the right boys," and we moved to the right. All the water was shooting out into the house walls, ceilings, floors, etc. My eyes began to burn at this stage, but I didn't say anything. My heart was beating a mile a minute, it seemed. All the time we were in the house, I felt myself inching forward on the hose. After about ten minutes, which seemed like an eternity, the room cleared. There was no more smoke. But-there were no more firemen either! Just Ted and me holding on to the water hose, which was still spewing water. I got mad and told Ted, "pull back on that handle on the hose and let's get out of here!" When Ted pulled back on the handle on the nozzle, the water quit coming out of the fire hose. We threw down the hose and went outside. Outside, the people were clapping, yelling and laughing all at the same time. At a distance, I saw the old firemen coughing and hacking. I kind of felt sorry for them. Ted and I went home, smelling of smoke. We took a bath and put on clean clothes. There you have it. I was a fireman for a day! That evening I went to the movies like as if nothing had happened.

After the fire incident, whenever there was a fire, I kept my distance. I joined the rest of the people and became a 'looky-loo'.

My job at the Ice Plant was quite interesting. I didn't work making ice. I helped deliver it. I was a 'Swamper', for the driver. In other words, he and I delivered the ice to the houses, the only difference between me and the diver was that he drove the truck. When I was first hired out, one of the first questions Bill Humphries, my boss asked me was, "Do you know how to drive a truck?" I lied, saying "Yes, I do." He hired me. I lived on Chihuahua Hill, for Christ's sake, we were poor, when was I to get money to buy a car or truck--- never, but I needed a job and I got it!

Charlie Salas, the man I worked with taught me how to drive, on the job. We started work at the plant at seven in the morning. Charlie would get the truck out of the garage, which was adjacent to the plant and back it to the dock. The Ice Plant Operator would feed three hundred pound blocks through the "scoring machine" and on to the dock. The ice would come through a square opening which had a door, when we loaded the truck. Once the truck was loaded, we would close the door to the opening and drive off.

The ice was scored about an inch deep. The block had two fifty-pound pieces and eight twenty-five pound pieces. It came out of the hole in one piece. W would take our ice picks, which we carried in scabbards on our belts and we would pick into the scored areas, either getting a twenty-five pound chunk, a fifty-pound piece or even a one hundred-pound piece, whatever the customer wanted.

When it was 'ice day', for the different neighborhoods, the people would put a red cardboard somewhere in front of their house so that we could see it. This cardboard was about one foot square. One corner of it was white. Whichever that portion of white was pointing, that determined how much ice they wanted. We delivered ice to the business section of town first, the restaurants, the bars, the local clubs. There was always somebody there at these places, straightening things up, stocking their beer cases, cleaning their bars from the previous days doings. After that, we would do our 'route'. We had a different section of town that we delivered to every day. We delivered to Old Bisbee, Lowell, Bakerville and Warren. Most of our customers were in Old Bisbee. Hardly any in Warren area. Warren in those days was considered the 'Knob Hill of Bisbee'. They already had refrigerators, while Old Bisbee folks still clung to their "ice boxes".

It was neat delivering ice to the houses. We would holler, "Ice Man" and go into their kitchen, put whatever weight of ice they wanted into the ice box, get the money, which was "always" on top of the ice box and go to the next house. I venture to say that three fourths of the time we wouldn't even see our customers, but the money was always there on top of the ice box. The customers were the best I must say. There was a big three story boarding house on O.K. Street called, "The Brooks Apartments". It seems like all the apartments wanted ice. They all took twenty-five pounds for their ice boxes. Charlie Salas, my partner, would deliver ice to the ground floor. I would take a 'scored' hundred pound block on by back and a fifty-pound block hanging on tongs on one of arms. I would climb to the second floor landing, leaving the 100-pound block there and continue to the third floor with the 50-pound chunk. After serving the top floor, I would then go back to the second floor to deliver the ice to those apartments. It beat going back and forth to the truck every trip. I was nineteen at the time, full of piss and vinegar, so I could handle what I was doing. Doing the ice route every day really built my legs and stamina. It helped me tremendously playing sports. I never got tired.

I worked at the Ice Plant for sometime until I got to be an 'Ice Plant Operator'. An operator makes ice, waits on customers that come to the dock for ice and also loads the trucks. I worked at this until Arizona Edison Company, the owner, sold it, then I was transferred to the 'Bull Gang'. At Arizona Edison Company, I worked in the electric department as a 'Grunt'. On the gas and water department I worked as a ditch digger, a repairman and whatever else they had. I enjoyed it! Doing this type of work helped me in my later years at my job.

As you may have assessed by now, I was very sports oriented in my youth. I played baseball, softball, basketball and even bowled in the local league here in Bisbee, Arizona. One day, our basketball team, a team composed of guys my age, went to Ajo, Arizona to play a game at the invitation of some guy in Ajo. None of my teammates nor I had ever been to Ajo. Nevertheless, here we were. We were met at the gym, by a man who guided us to a dressing room. We came out of the dressing room and went in the gym. There we got the surprise of our lives! Sitting in the bleachers, which by the way were packed, sat people young and old who were all Indians. No, they didn't have feathers, but Indians none the less. Sure enough, you guessed it, our opponents were a bunch of young Indian guys. That game turned out to be one of the roughest games I'd ever played in. The only referee in the game was Indian. He let the game get out of hand. I ended up getting a bloody nose. A couple of our players got kicked out for scuffling with the opponents. A few fouled out. We won the low scoring game, 44 to 43 and we were booed as we left the floor. We showered, dressed and left for our cars and----surprise! Everything was white! It had snowed while we played. Everything was covered with about four inches of snow. We slowly drove out of town. We finally arrived in the friendly confines of our homes. I couldn't sleep that night. All night long I kept thinking about Indians!

WINNING A RACE

I have pleasant memories of when I was a young man. Seems like my fondest memories were of festive days like the fourth of July, Armistice Day, Thanksgiving Day and yes, Easter.

I was in my early twenties on this particular Fourth of July. I got up early, put on some dress clothes, because after all, it was a National Holiday. I went to Brewery Gulch to see the famous "Hill Climb", which was staged every year for sometime now. The "Hill" in question is a mountain which is directly in front of the bars on Brewery Gulch. For years the Encinas Family, consisting of the father and three sons, would dominate this particular race, with the father winning the race most of the time. Sure enough, on this Fourth of July, the winner was the father, followed closely by his two sons, then the rest of the participants. Mr. Encinas, I would say, was in his late 40s or early 50s, but he was in perfect shape. Why wouldn't he be? After all, he worked for the City of Bisbee Sanitation Department, going up and down the mountains in Bisbee, picking up garbage and putting it into a big canvas bag which he carried on his back, much like Santa Clause. When the canvas bag was full, he would take it to the street, get another canvas bag and continue to get garbage from the houses and put it in his bag. So, yes, he was a good athlete when it came to climbing this Hill on the Fourth of July.

THE COPPER PICK

The student body of Douglas High School came up with the idea of a Trophy to be given to the winner of the Thanksgiving Day football game. The copper was mined in Bisbee at that time, smelted in Douglas, this formed the Copper Pick Trophy. The graduating class of 1945 was the First recipient of this award.

In the year 1944, Bisbee football season, we played a pretty good bunch of high schools. We played Tucson High School twice. We played Douglas High School on Armistice Day and won 20 to 19, in Douglas. Then we played again on Thanksgiving Day and beat Douglas for the second time by a score of 21 to 6. We only had 21 members on our team. There was a War on and most of the students had left school to enlist in the Armed Services.

Because of a previous football injury on my right shoulder, the coach used a whole roll of adhesive tape and taped my right arm to my body, to where I could not use but one arm. But—before the First Quarter had ended, the tape had come loose with my body sweat. Then I used two arms to tackle. Douglas High School had a bigger team, but us "Mountain Goats" beat those Douglas "Smoke Chokers".

We had such a small (quantity) team, that we had to play both offense and defense. Nowadays, on group plays offense and another group play defense only.

In the spring, we had an assembly and members of the DHS Student Body came to BHS and we presented the "Copper Pick Trophy". I am very proud to have been on the winning team and of being the recipient of the very first Copper Pick.

Recently, I received a phone call to be at Bisbee High School, in reference to the "Pick". When I got there, I met four other players from the1944 squad. There was Dan Vucurevich, Jack Craig, George Bugen and "Sikes" Hendricks. My other teammates were scattered all over the U.S. and some are deceased.

ARMISTICE DAY –1944 FOOTBALL

Bisbee High School and Douglas High School have the second longest high school rivalry in the United States. Two schools in Connecticut have the longest.

November 11, 1944, the Douglas Football Team came to Bisbee to play in the Annual Armistice Day Game. The Warren Ball Park was overflowing with fans from both towns. The weather was pleasant enough, nice and mild for being a November Day.

The reason I am writing about this particular game is that on that day, although Bisbee beat Douglas 20 to 19, its not about the score, it's about a play, which I cannot (some 60 years later) get out of my mind. It gnaws at me.

It was the waning minutes of the game and Douglas has the ball on Bisbee's seven yard line, fourth down and goal. Before the game had started, our Coach, Waldo Dicus said to the Linemen, "If a pass comes in your direction, bat it down. Do you understand?? BAT IT DOWN!!" Well, here it is, fourth down and Wayne Huish, a big 6'2", 210 pound Fullback, fades back to pass. The Defensive right side of our line rushes him and forces him to go backwards while looking for an open Receiver. He flings the ball right to where I am standing. I could read the spiral on the ball. In that instant I saw the ball, the nearest Defender, who was about eight yards from me and more importantly, I saw 93 yards of open field, intercepting the pass and scoring! But then I remembered our Coach's words, "You Linemen, if a pass comes your way, "BAT IT DOWN, BAT IT DOWN!!" We took over on downs, marched from the seven-yard line to our own thirty-five and the gun sounded, ending the game! Even now, at an elderly age, I think of what might have been. I could have intercepted that pass easily, run ninety-three yards for a touchdown, had my name in the record books credited with the longest interception for a touchdown by a Defensive Lineman. Sometimes it just doesn't pay to be obedient.

THANKSGIVING DAY – 1944
FOOTBALL

We went to Douglas on Thanksgiving Day, but the game was postponed. Too much rain. Bummer!! We waited until the following Saturday to play the Turkey Day Game.

Our coach, seeing that we barely beat Douglas on Armistice Day had a feeling that their Coach might have something "cooking" for the Thanksgiving Day Game...and it wasn't Turkey.

In those days' we practiced from three to 6:30 P.M.. By 6:30, the day would turn to dark in November. We would practice with and against a five and six man lines. Around 6 o'clock, Dicus our Coach, would look around very suspiciously and then would practice our "Two Linemen Defense", when it got dark. The Coach feared that Douglas had someone peering at us with binoculars from, "Cheapskate Road", a dirt road behind and above Warren Ball Park. So we practiced the two men's defenses in semi-darkness for fear Douglas might see it.

Below is the formation:

```
            Bailich--------> <---------Dabovich
                      X              X    X
                 X                        X
                                          X
            X

                                              X


                 X
```

Game time came. Dushan Balich played Right Tackle and I played Left Tackle. When Douglas came to the line of scrimmage, we showed them a 5-man Defensive Line, thusly: XXXXX.

Just before they snap the ball, three of our guys, that were inside the two Tackles dropped back a couple of yards. The Douglas Offensive Line sees this: Balich   Dabovich

              X   X   X

When the ball is snapped, Balich and I throw ourselves toward each other creating confusion in the line. The three guys who have dropped back a couple of yards, have a field day coming up to make tackles at the line of scrimmage!

Here is what happened:

Left Tackle	Balich–><–Dabovich
^ ^ ^	
Interior Linemen	X X X
^ ^ ^	
Inside Linebackers	X X X
^	^
Outside Linebackers X	X
^ ^ ^	
Safety	X

This went on all afternoon. We beat them handily! We (Balich or I) didn't have rib pads like kids have now, nor face-guards on helmets to protect our faces, nothing like that.

I got home that afternoon, sore, hurting all over, but very happy!!

REMEMBERING WALLACE'S POOL HALL

There was a Scoreboard on th wall at Wallace's Pool Hall. I used to fill in the scores from the 16 Major League Teams on Saturdays and Sundays. Since I worked at Arizona Edison, (Arizona Public Service) Monday through Friday, old man Wallace would copy the scores, which came over a Ticker-Tape Machine that was located next to the wall. Mr. Wallace would pay me to keep score on weekends. The Majors didn't play night games in those days. They played 154 games way back then. Now there are 32 teams in the Majors and each team plays 162 games in a season. Back then Double Headers were played on Sundays. Although the season started the first week in April, it was over on th last day of September, with the World Series beginning two to three days later. Now the season ends, payoffs begin, the World Series is played and it's over---- in October, close to Halloween. Ridiculous!

There was a black man by the name of Fred Hollingsworth. Fred owned the San Sue Café up on Brewery Gulch. All the blacks would congregate there to eat. Fred leased the back of Wallace's Pool Hall. He made the best Chili Beans at Wallace's, mmmm they were really good! Fred had just about all of Bisbee coming in the Pool Hall, not to shoot pool, but to eat his Chile!

When my younger brother John was hired to work at Wallace's, that gave Mr. Wallace time to come in later. Mrs. Wallace (Helen) also worked there. The people liked her a lot. Although the guys would not buy the nude photo magazines or condoms when she was behind the counter.

All the young guys my age liked to "hang out" at Wallace's just to get out of the house. It was a good time back then all right!

THE "ICE CARD"

The "Ice" customers were given a 12" square card which was placed on a window or door facing the street. The card was 3/4 red, with one corner white. The Iceman would look for the white corner of the card to lt him know the amount of ice they wanted. For example: If the white corner was facing up that meant that the customer didn't want any ice. If the white corner was facing left, that customer wanted 25 pounds of ice. If the white corner was facing down, the customer wanted 50 pounds of ice. If the white corner was facing right, the amount of ice wanted was 75 pounds. That way, the iceman would look for the card and see where the white corner was facing. He would then get the ice tongs on the proper block of ice and take it to the customer.

Some customers were hardly ever home. They would leave the door unlocked so that the iceman could come in with the ice. The money for the ice was there for the iceman to take. He would take the money and leave and so it went, from one customer to another. People were so trusting in those days.

It was hard work, but I was young and strong. I really didn't mind going up the hills and steps. It gave me a good workout.

ICE CAPADES

My first "real" job after finishing high school was delivering ice to the customers that didn't have a refrigerator. They had "Ice boxes". I used to deliver 25 pounds to a lady that lived at the end of Tombstone Canyon. She would melt the ice and wash her hair in the water from the melted ice. She would do this ritual every other day. She claimed that this method would keep her hair from turning gray. Ha! I saw her one year later and yep...gray.

There was a restaurant in upper Brewery Gulch owned by a black family. I would deliver ice and place it in an open Coca Cola Box full of sodas, standing upright. After placing the ice on top of the sodas, I would get my ice pick out o my scabbard to break the ice chunk into small pieces in the Coca Cola Box. Because I am left handed one black lady wouldn't come near me because she said I was possessed by the devil. She would not come near me at all! Oh well.

I delivered a 25-pound piece of ice to a nice looking black lacy who had a very narrow opening in her Ice Box. I had to chisel the chunk of ice to make it fit in the Box. Normally, no one was home at this house, however, on this day, the lady was home. She saw me "trimming" the ice and exclaimed in aloud voice, "Mr. Iceman, if she don't fit, don't fo'ce it". I broke the chunk in two, put it in the Ice Box and left.

There was an old grouch of a woman in Warren, who took 50 pounds every other day. I had to take off my shoes, take the ice in a special bag, so as not t drip water on her kitchen floor. She would stay there watching me put the ice in her Ice Box to make sure I didn't make a mess. I hated going to that house. She finally died and went to Heaven. Poor St. Peter.

I was working at the Ice Plant, located in Lowell by the Cemetery, making ice, at the same time waiting on customers that drove up to buy ice from the dock. Every other day a man from cross the line (Naco, Mexico), would drive up in a beat up old truck, back up to the dock, get out of his truck and say to me, "I want a thousand pounds of ....ice." This happened every other day, the same thing, "I want a thousand pounds of ...ice. One of the days that he came, I was in a bad mood. When he said.... "of ice", I told him, "Mister, that's all we sell here". After that he would come in and say, "A thousand pounds, please". I said to myself, "Aw right!"

One day I delivered some ice to a house in Warren where there were maybe three women and three men playing cards. I put the ice in the Ice Box and was on my way out, when one of he guys said to me, "So you're the Iceman"? I answered, "Yes Sir". Then he says, "And my wife is pregnant". I didn't know what to say, when all of a sudden all of them broke out in laughter. I left that house embarrassed....and mad. I continued to deliver ice to that house, but I never saw anybody there.

THE MISSING PLAYER

I was coaching a Babe Ruth Team at the Warren Ball Park. One day I noticed all the action stopped. The Umpire came over to the dugout and asked, "where's your batter Coach"? I looked at my score book and yelled the name of the kid that was supposed to be batting. One of the players, "he left the dugout about five minutes ago, Coach". I went out of the dugout to look around the area between the grandstand and the third base bleachers. I saw my player coming from the restroom area zipping up his pants. I asked him, "where have you been man?" He very calmly replied, "I just had to go Coach". He grabbed a bat and very nonchalantly walked to home plate to bat. I looked up into the stands. The people there did not have an inkling of an idea what had just transpired. Kids...very unpredictable.

Another time at the same ball park, we were in a scoreless struggle with the opposing team. We had men on the bases. One of our better hitters was going to bat in a few minutes. When, while sitting in the dugout, I saw a pair of womens legs walking in front of the dugout. The lady stops, bends down to look into the dugout, spots her son and says, "You have to go home now, Zack. You have a violin lesson this afternoon". The kid changes shoes and walks out of the dugout. I am flabbergasted!! I have to send my only scrub I have on the bench to bat in place of the good hitter, who had just left to practice on his fiddle. The pinch hitter promptly struck out, thank you and the inning was over. We eventually won the low scoring game, but we had to earn it because our slugger had left to fiddle away in the afternoon.

CLASS "D" BASEBALL

If I have a weakness, it's the sport of Baseball. While attending school at Central School, I used to watch the older kids playing baseball in the playground during recess. I was too young to play, but, I would fantasize that someday I would be big enough to be playing baseball and some little kid would be watching me play, just as I did when I was his age.

We had a huge Fig Tree in our front yard. I would get on the roof of our house, then jump onto the Fig Tree, sit there to listen to the baseball games that would be broadcast from the Warren Ball Park. We didn't own a radio, however, our neighbor across the steps from us did. The man would listen to the radio just about every day. I would be up there in our Fig Tree, listening to the announcer broadcast the afternoons game. Bisbee was in a class "D" Baseball League. They were called the Bisbee Bees. I vaguely remember some of the names of the Bees on that team. I remember a player whose name was Joe La Piana and another whose name was Fay Starr. A boy by the name of Alex Kellner was from Tucson, who was a pitcher for the Tucson Cowboys. Kellner was only 16 years old and he was playing pro ball already. He later went up to the Major Leagues, where he pitched for the Philadelphia Athletics of the American League.

In those days there were only sixteen teams in the Majors. Eight in the National League and eight in the America League. Now, there 16 teams in the National and 14 in the America League. Progress!!

There were some really good ball players' in those days. One pitcher who wasn't only good, but was very popular as well was Jesse Flores. He later pitched several years with the Philadelphia A's in the American

League. Although this league was classified as "D", it was a good league. The ball players played better than the Class "C" players of now a days.

Carl Morris owned the local radio station, KSUN and he would broadcast the games on the radio. Morris used to "murder" the Spanish language, call the ball "peloto", instead of "pelota". On one blustery, windy day he said on the air, "There's a fly ball hit to deep center field, the second baseman comes under it for the out". He reminded me of Dizzy Dean when he would broadcast the game of the day. For example; one broadcast day, he was explaining the action this way. "There is a runner on first and the batter gets a hit and the runner from first "slud" into third base. What he should have said was that the runner "slid" into third base. The "slud" remark made headlines all over the United States. He was such an icon that it was accepted as correct whatever he said. He sure "murdered" the English" language as well. When the Cardinals were to play in the World Series, Dizzy said that "me and Paul" would pitch and win for the Cardinals. Paul was his brother. He should have said "Paul and I" instead, but people did not bother correcting him because, like I said, he was so popular that nobody contradicted him.

ANTS

My father was involved in giving out commodities at the old Franklin School Building on Opera Drive. The big building was no longer a school. Once a month, commodities such as powdered milk, cheese and the like were distributed to poor people at the building. I don't know if my Dad was in charge of the project there or a volunteer or what his capacity was. I was only ten, maybe eleven at the time. My brother Ted and I used to go there and play around in the field at the old school. As a child my legs hurt all the time like rheumatism. One day my brother and I went to the Franklin building to be with our Dad. I was in no mood to play, so I just stood around. While standing there in the dirt field, I felt a different kind of pain in both my legs. I looked down, to where I was standing, lo and behold, I was standing on an ant hill!

Well, let me tell you, that pain that I felt on my legs was different from the dull ache I felt every day that I actually welcomed it. I stood on that ant hill for what seemed to be an eternity. Finally I walked away stomping my feet and hitting my pant legs to get rid of the ants that were still on me. The ache from the ant stings hurt me the rest of the day. I went home not saying anything about my ordeal. The next morning, I got up and the ant stings did not hurt anymore! More importantly, the rheumatism ache on my legs was Gone!!! That was the last time I ever suffered from that awful ache. I think that the ant stings did it. Maybe that is the best "medicine" to cure rheumatic aches in the legs, I don't know, but it sure worked for me! Thanks to the lowly ant.

AT THE CIRCUS

My Dad worked for the WPA when we were children. There were seven of us kids but one of my bothers died when he was eight years old of Double Pneumonia. We didn't own a car, so everywhere we went, we went on foot. One day my eldest sister, myself and Ted were going to school. Two other brothers and my youngest sister had not started school yet. In school, we found out that a Circus was coming to town over the weekend. We were all excited at my house because we had never been to a Circus. Except what we had read in books, we had no idea what a Circus was. My Mother told us not to raise our hopes about going to the Circus because we were limited as far as money was concerned.

My elder sister and I were relentless with our Mother to please, please take us. Finally my Mother said, "Okay, we will go Saturday evening". We could hardly wait for Saturday, but we did. Finally, Saturday was here. We asked Dad if he wanted to go. He said, "No". Dad was a homebody. When he worked he had to walk to his work place, then walk home in the evening, so he was never in the mood to go anywhere after he came home from work.

Around six o'clock on Saturday evening, my mother, sister, brother and I started walking from Chihuahua Hill, five miles to the Circus site. My younger brother and sister were too small to go, so they stayed home with Dad. The five mile walk to me, didn't seem long, after all we were going to the Circus! As we approached the Circus ground, my heart began to pound with excitement! We saw bright colored lights, thousands of light bulbs, multicolored triangle type flags waving in the evening breeze. People were approaching the big brown Circus Tent from all angles. Cars, lots of cars, were driving there, some beeping their horns at the hordes of people who were converging on the Circus.

My family stood at the opening of the Big Tent. We could hear music coming from within this huge tent. People were buying tickets from a real small ticket place, which was positioned directly in front of the tent. My brother, sister and I stood in awe of everything. We wanted to go in, but my Mother said, "All right, lets go home now". We didn't argue with her. We started to walk back home, five miles away.

When we got home, we went straight to bed and had a good nights sleep. Why not? We had walked 10 miles to and from the Circus. We didn't go in, but our Mother had kept her promise. She took us to the Circus and we were satisfied.

It would be many, many years before we finally go to actually go into a Circus Tent!

AT THE MOVIES

I was quite a movie goer as a young man. I would go to the movies on Sunday, Tuesday and Friday at 7:00 p.m. every week. If a movie was already started, I would never go in to see it. I always made it a point to be at the theater at least 15 minutes before te lights went out and the movie would start.

The best movies were always shown on Tuesdays, Wednesdays and Thursdays, then the marquis would change for the Friday movie. On Saturday, the movie was usually a western or a kid picture. I never went on Saturdays because all he kids would go. They would constantly go in and out of the theater, run around, yell and raise all kinds of hell. I know because I took my older sister's son Perry, because he wanted to see Hop-Along Cassidy. It was a double feature. To me it was a living hell, but my nephew was having a ball, although, Perry wasn't a hell raiser like the rest of the hell cats at the show.

I used to go to the matinee movies, but when I came out of the darkened theater into sunlight...wow, I would get a strong, bright, flashing light in my eyes. Most of the time, it would result in headaches. That is why I quit going to the movies during the day.

When I would go to the movies, I would sit in the same seat on the bottom floor. All the years that I went to the show at the Lyric Theater, I never went upstairs to the balcony. I was watching a movie on night, it was one of those movies that captivated the audience. All of a sudden this high school kid, who was up in the balcony shouts really loud, "Mother", everyone in the hushed crowd began to laugh. I found out later that the attendant and the manager found him out and removed him from the theater. I think about that incident, even now, and I break out into a laugh. I just make sure nobody is around for fear that they might think I'm looney.

Another time while watching a movie, someone who was sitting in the balcony inflated a condom and let it go. There were some girls sitting in the row in front of me when the condom dropped on one of the girls' lap. She took the inflated condom in her hands and said to the girls that were with her, "Look girls, someone threw this balloon from the balcony". One of the girls whispered something in the girl's ear while the others snickered. All of a sudden, the girl with the "balloon", let out a yell and threw it away from her! By this time the people around that area had got wind of what was going on. There was quite a lot of laughter for a short period of time. The girl in question, just covered her face with her hands in embarrassment.

My favorite movie stars at the time were Claudette Colbert and Jean Arthur. Not because of their acting, but because of their beauty.

BOY SCOUTS

A lot of things I experienced as a Boy Scout. I will write on a few of them.

I had a friend about my age. He was an American citizen of Mexican descent. He asked me at school on day if it was possible for him to join the Boy Scouts. Sure enough, that night we had our meeting. I asked my Scoutmaster about my friend wanting to join the Boy Scots. The Scoutmaster said, "Sure, just tell your friend to come to the meeting next week and we will go from there". I thanked him. Next morning I told my friend. He was elated! The following week as I approached the place where we are to have our meeting, there was my friend, beaming with a really happy face on him. He went in with me. I introduced him to the Scoutmaster. The Scoutmaster looked at him and said, "We are going to have to vote to see if you can become a Boy Scout". I was stunned! I spoke up. I asked the Scoutmaster, "Why are we to vote to see if my friend can join the Boy Scouts. Nobody voted when I joined". He answered, "That's the way it is". Needless to say, we voted. The vote was unanimous by all the boys at te meeting, to have him join. The boy was happy and we all left the hall.

When I got home, I told my parents what had happened. Both Mom and Dad asked if the boy was an American boy. I answered, "Yes, but of Mexican blood". My Dad got upset and angry, turned to my Mother he said, "Prejudice! It is still here and it always will be here. The reason this particular boy was admitted into the scouts is because the other scouts aren't prejudiced yet". That is when I first experienced prejudice. It wasn't too long after that happened that I quit the Boy

Scouts. My dad said that my Scout activities were interfering with my chores at home.

It would be years later before I fully understood why we had to vote to admit someone into the Boy Scouts.

While in the Scouts, I participated in raising the United States Flag on Bucky O'Neil Hill on the Fourth of July. The evening before, on July 3rd, I told my Mother, "We have to raise the flag tomorrow when the sun rises and we have to lower it at sundown". Since I didn't own a watch, my mother and I worked out a plan as to when we would take the flag down on the Fourth.

Early on the Fourth, two other boys and I went up Bucky O'Neil Hill and raised the Flag on a flag pole, which had been there for years. We came down the hill and said we would meet at a certain time that evening and take the Flag down. We went to the events throughout the day. When it came time, we met at te Post Office and started climbing the mountain. When we got to the top where the Flag was, I told the other boys to look toward my house and look for a bed sheet. My Mother's plan was that as soon as the sun went down, she and my big sister would go outside and unfurl a big white bed sheet, that would be the signal to lower the Flag. Then we would come on down. Sure enough, one of the boys spotted "something white". I looked and the big white sheet looked the size of a postage stamp. We lowered the Flag, came down the mountain and went home.

No one was aware what all was involved in Flag raising, but us young kids surely did.

THANKSGIVING ON CHIHUAHUA HILL

While living on Chihuahua Hill during my preteen years, I remember about when Thanksgiving Day was approaching.

My Dad worked at a meat market owned by two bachelor brothers, Mike and Lee Jovanovich. I would venture to say they were in their 50's in my young eyes. On the day before Thanksgiving the Jovanovich brothers would give all of their employees a fresh turkey.

About four days before Thanksgiving my Mother would take slices of bread, put them on a tray, leave the tray outside so the bread would dry. After a day in the sun, Mom would bring the "bread tray" in and let it set for three days until the bread was nice and dry. Mom would "crumb" the bread to use as the homemade dressing for our Thanksgiving Dinner.

In boiling water Mom would cook the turkey gizzard, liver, heart and neck part. After all these parts were cooked, she would cut them up in small pieces. She would mix chopped celery and other stuff with the crumbs from the bread. She would add other stuff too, other then what I mentioned, but being a boy, I didn't hang around the kitchen too much so I don't know what all she put in there. All I know is that when it came to dinnertime, I think I liked her stuffing more then the turkey!

Mother would set the dining table with her finest linen tablecloth, set the turkey on the center of the table, just like in the movies. We would sit around our round table. My Dad, even though he was not a religious man would say "Grace". Now as an adult, I still remember that particular scene, day and moment that my Dad showed some religious traits.

We would take our time eating. We all had a "Feast" every Thanksgiving. The food aroma coming from the kitchen filled the house. It smelled nice. The pumpkin pies, Mom also made from scratch. She would buy some pumpkins, cook them, add cinnamon, cloves, sugar and other spices. She would pour this mixture into the made from scratch pie crusts and bake them. The pies would be scrumptious!!

After dinner, I would look back at our table and see that poor old turkey. Nothing left but the carcass.

Nowadays, the lady of the house makes pumpkin pies from the Libby cans from already prepared pumpkins or buys the pies already made or frozen. They're good but home made is 100% better!!

Dressing today comes already put together in a box by "Mrs. Cubbison". It has bread, spices and I don't know what all. When my wife and I got married she used the already "boxed" stuffing. I sure did not like it. I told her that my mother made the stuffing from scratch. Since then, when we eat turkey, we have homemade stuffing and is it ever good!

Ah! Those were the good old days!!!

ALTER BOY

My mother was very strict with us. I would envy the kids in the neighborhood because they were out and about anytime of the day or night. Not us! We had to ask permission to go outside; for crying out loud!!! We had to do what she said and we did. We accepted it because at that time were taught that all kids did as they were told. Were we naive? Ha!!

My mother was a strict Catholic. She decided that I should be an Altar Boy. I didn't want to be, but she was the boss, so I became an Altar Boy at Sacred Heart Catholic Church in Bisbee. Seems like I was always at church. I knew the church grounds by heart, that's how much time I spent there. I had to put on that "dress looking outfit" over my clothes and light the candles, move the big old book that Father read from one side of the Altar to the other side. I liked to pull on the rope to ring the bell announcing that the services were about to start. I would pull on the rope at three different intervals. That was fun! I also passed the collection plate, which I liked doing the most because I could exercise my legs, plus see how much money the congregation put in the collection basket.

I remember doing a lot of kneeling. Jesus Christ, did we kneel a lot! I don't remember how I got out of the Altar Boy thing, but it was an experience that I still remember now that I am an adult.

ACORNS

During the summer around July or early Aught my mother and us kids would go to visit Mrs. Sophia Ruiz, who lived in a house on Dubaker Canyon. Eventually the conversation would turn to "bellotas" (bay-o-tas)...Acorns. Both ladies liked and enjoyed eating the bellotas, or in English; Acorns.

During our visit there, Mrs. Ruiz got a blanket. With the blanket in her arms and Mom carrying a cloth bag, we all left the house walking toward the mountains close by. When we got there, I saw dozens of Oak Trees. Mrs. Ruiz took the blanket and spread it under one of the Oak Trees. She then said, "Chrisito, (that's me) climb up this tree and shake some of the branches". I did as she said. Pretty soon, Acorns started "raining" down to the ground on the spread out blanket. I came down from the tree to help gather the fallen Acorns into a cloth bag. It took a long time to fill the bag, but after a while it was full of Acorns.

Mrs. Ruiz picked up her blanket, shook it then folded it. We walked back to her house, my mother carried the Acorns and Mrs. Ruiz carried the blanket. At Mrs. Ruiz' house, she and my mother each got their share of Acorns. After that we would go to Mrs. Ruiz' house and go "bellota hunting". The people in the neighborhood got wind of the Acorn harvest. They wanted to buy some from Mrs. Ruiz. Mrs. Ruiz sold them the Acorns and made a small profit for herself that summer.

Most people don't like Acorns, but some do. Acorns are kind of sour, but they are good. I like them myself.

This is the way to eat an Acorn: put one between your teeth to cut it in half. You get the yellow to orange colored "meat" out, eat it as you throw the Acorn Shell away. Some Acorns have a yellow worm in them, so before you eat one, look it over, otherwise you will have chewed the Acorn with the worm.

My little sister, Christina used to take a cut shell, put it between her forefinger and middle finger, blow into the shell to make a loud piercing whistling sound. She enjoyed making that annoying sound!

HUMOR - IT'S WONDERFUL

One night our baseball team went to Douglas to play a game. The games usually started when it got dark, about 8:00 p.m.. We left Bisbee in several cars about 6:00 p.m.. Since it only takes about a half hour to go from Bisbee to Douglas, we arrived there in plenty of time. The car I was in also had our manager in it. When we were pulling into Douglas on G Avenue, close to the Gadsden Hotel, our manager told the driver to pull over to the curb, right in front of the hotel. The car behind us, with the other fellows in it, pulled over to the curb as well. We got out of our cars and stood there on the sidewalk. Our manager told us, "Listen fellows, just follow my lead. I want to see just how curious these Douglas people are down here." Looking up toward the sky, our manager started to point his finger skyward. We all followed suit. We all started looking skyward and pointing at nothing really. Soon people that were walking and cars going by would stop. People were getting out of there cars and looking up. Some, were even pointing in the direction that our manager was pointing. We looked around and started to smile at one another. The manager said "Okay boys, lets go to the ball park."

As we pulled away from the curb, I looked back and saw about a dozen people standing on the sidewalk, pointing skyward. Ah! Human nature, it's wonderful!

When I was nine years old, I fell in love with baseball. I would rather play baseball than go to the movies. I just liked playing Baseball that's all! At age 14 I stated playing organized ball

One night, we had a league game at Horace Mann Court. This was long before the field was converted into a swimming pool and parking lot. I played first base and a boy by the name of Alex Ayala played second base. Bucky Cobb played short stop and Donald Reak played third base. It was a decent infield group. We were going along really good when a batter hits a towering pop up in the infield. Our third baseman, our shortstop, our second baseman and I all ran toward second base, all hollering, "I GOT IT!" Just as the ball was coming down, Bucky yells, "YOU TAKE IT ALEX!" Alex looked up and the ball hit him squarely on his forehead and bounced over into left field. I ran over to my position, the batter who had hit the ball circled the bases as the left fielder chased the ball. I looked over toward the shortstop position and there was Bucky rolling on the ground, laughing his fool head off and pointing at our second baseman, who by now had an enormous bump on his head.

The batter had himself a home run on Alex's "Heady" play!

MANAGING BASEBALL

I stopped playing baseball and softball at the age of 40. The reason being that my legs told me, "Quit!" My brain was telling me that I was running at full speed, when the truth of the matter was, I was just running and not with any speed.

Since I couldn't get out of baseball just like that, I decided that I would help the younger people who were willing to play baseball. I started out managing a men's Fast Pitch Team. There were some very talented players and some not so hot ones. The good players, I didn't have to coach too much, although I would give them some pointers. It was the less talented ones whom I got the most pleasure in teaching.

I remember one guy who had never played in a league game or a sanctioned game in his life. Sure, he played games, but they were of the, "pick-up", or neighborhood variety. I got a hold of this kid and basically had to show him how to hold the bat properly, how to stand in the Batters Box and how to, "unlock" his hips when he was about to hit the ball. This guy, although saying he knew how to play baseball, didn't. This player was about 26 years of age and a fast learner. The poor guy wanted to be an outfielder. I told him to get his ass out to the outfield, that I would hit him some balls. Well, to tell you the truth, it was comical to watch him "corral" a routine fly ball. He would come in on the ball, then go out and finally "jump" to get it. The ball would be about chest high when he would jump for it. He was a good listener. He turned out to be one of the better hitters and fielders of the whole league after he finished his first year. Even now when I see him, he thanks me for the help I gave him. That makes me feel like Tony The Tiger—JUST "GREEAAT!!"

One time our team wasn't complete for a certain game we were going to play and I had to play a "Bench Warmer." When it was his turn to bat, I told him not to swing at a 3 and 0 count. Well, he worked the count to three balls and no strikes, when on the very next pitch he swings and knocks the ball out of the ball park for a home run. He is grinning as he rounds the bases. His teammates meet him at home plate to congratulate him. I'm sitting in the dugout fuming! Don't get me wrong, I appreciate runs and winning, but I hate when somebody disobeys what I tell them.

When all the players came back to the dugout, I got up to seek my "home run" hitter. I asked him, "What did I tell you when you went to bat?" He answered, "You told me that not even Major Leaguers swing at a 3 and 0 pitch, except maybe Ted Williams." I finally congratulated him, but not before I read him the riot act. You see, nine out of ten times when the count is three balls and no strikes, the very next pitch will be a ball. Why? Well, there are several reasons: One, could be that the pitcher is wild. Two, the pitcher wants to get a strike in so bad, that he aims the ball instead of pitching it. Three, sometimes a pitcher might have command of all his pitches, then all of a sudden, his control deserts him. It happens.

We were playing a pretty good soldier all-star team at Fort Huachuca one time. There was a pitcher from another team that I got to pitch for us. Like I do before every game, I talk to the team and go over the signs I will be giving them during the game. In this particular game the bases were loaded, up to bat was "our pitcher." He had worked the count to 3 and 2. There were two outs, I yelled at the batter to look at me and I gave him the "take" sign. The pitch comes in, the batter swings and misses by a mile. The inning is over, the rally squelched and I'm going bonkers! I called the pitcher over and asked him, "Why did you swing at that pitch? It was way outside the strike zone." He answered, "I thought you were giving me the Home Run sign." I said, "You!!" I went to the dugout cussing and fuming! It's all humorous to me now, but not at the time. I'a stickler for rules an I wanted my players to adhere to them to the letter while they are under my command. That is why I have always had winning teams.

One time in Little League, the league decided t have a Tournament after the league was over. Our best pitcher came to the ball park stating he couldn't play because he had a headache. I told him to sit down. Most of these kids are 10, 11 and 12 years old and most are still babies in their thinking. I then rewrote the whole line-up. I started our short stop, put my second baseman at short and a kid that had never played in the infield all season, at second.

The game started. It was going along smoothly, thank you, when with two outs, our pitcher got wild and loaded the bases. I called time out to talk to the pitcher. The pitcher told me that his arm felt "tired", so I told him to go to short stop. Then I motioned to the short stop, who incidently was my son, to come in to pitch. My son is an infielder. He had never pitched in Little League before. The batter was a BIG kid, bigger then a twelve year old should be. He was tall, big broad shoulders, big ass, just B:IG! I told my son, "Get this guy out!" I walked to the dugout and sat down. The very first pitch is hit high, deep into center field. I stood up and watched in amazement as our little center fielder goes high into the sky and brings that sucker down for the third out! I breathe a sign of relief and seek out my son. He was more nervous than I was! Here I send him out to pitch, he's never pitched before and to top it off, he didn't even warm up his arm! The kid that had the headache came to me and said, "Mr. Dabovich, my headache is gone and I can pitch now if you want me to." I answered, "Hell yeah! Get your skinny ass out there and get those guys out!" He goes out, strikes out the side and preserves our win.

The fans came over to congratulate me on some "terrific coaching". Yeah —right. Sometime managing a team isn't all a manager does. For example: One night I took the team to Douglas, Az to play a league game, in the league we were in. We were in a Fast Pitch Softball League down there. There were eight teams, one from Agua Prieta, Sonora, one from Bisbee and six from Douglas. About four were above average, including our team. The other four were mediocre at best. This particular night we were to play against one of the best teams. Our player's wives got the "bright Idea" that they would all sit in a group to cheer for us. I said, "That's great!" Since we were the visiting team, we came to bat first. As our first batter comes up to the plate, all hell breaks loose. The girls had brought whistles, cow bells, party noise makers, gongs, etc, etc...I don't know what else. Every time the Douglas pitcher pitched a ball they would all "sound off" with the damndest noise you ever heard! After a couple of innings of this, the Captain of their team, who was also the pitcher called Time and started talking to the Umpire and pointing toward our "cheering" section. The Umpire took off his mask and motioned toward our bench. I went out to see what he wanted. He told me, "If you don't control those people, I"m going to forfeit the game and give it to Douglas." I said, "Wait a minuet 'Blue', I am managing my ball club here in the field, I have nothing to do with the fans in the stands. As far as I'm concerned, they are just fans and they can cheer, boo or make as much racket as they want. They aren't out here in the field interfering." The Umpire was between a rock and a hard place. He didn't know what to do. He and the other manager hee-hawed for about five minutes. Finally he told the other guy. "He is right. He can't tell them what to do any more then you or I can, so 'Play Ball'!" The pitcher did an about face and pitched the rest of the game amid all the racket. Incidently, while the Ump and the Manager were discussing their little dilemma, I, very slyly sent one of my players over to the rooting section to advise them—to keep it up, which they did. We eventually won the game with our "tenth" man and we laughed all the way home. Later on I told the girls in a very tactful and nice way, not to "overstay" our welcome and they agreed. After that the girls used their voices to root and cheer for us.

Another incident, involving the same two teams arose about a week later. The same pitcher as before was pitching against us. He was striking everybody out! Our batters would come back to our dugout shaking their heads. I asked a couple of them, "What's going on?" All of them told me "He's really on tonight. That ball has really got a bend to it."

I couldn't figure it out until an inning later. One of our guys hit a foul ball that went into our dugout, I bent over, picked it up and "Bingo", I knew why their pitcher was dominating us. The ball was a regulation softball all right, but it was rubber coated! The pitcher could dig his fingers into the ball and make it do just about anything he wanted it to do. When the inning was over, I got a hold of our left fielder and told him, "If you catch a fly ball out there, get that ball and throw it out of the park as far as you can throw." He said, O.K.." Now right behind the left field fence, there in Douglas is a Cemetery. Keep that in mind.

That next inning when their batter flied out to our left fielder for the third out, (I don't know why for the life of me, I chose the left fielder to get of the ball), sure enough, our left fielder waited a couple of seconds, turned toward the Cemetery and threw the ball out of the park. We all came in. I told the guys not to say anything. Sure enough, the Pitchers on their team started to scream, "Hey Coach, where's the ball?" I replied, "How should I know." The Umpire got a ball out of his bag and threw it t the pitcher. We were watching to see how the pitcher would react. Sure enough, the pitcher on their team started squawking right away. "That's not the ball I was pitching with. Where's the ball I was using?"I said, "Why are you asking me for? I'm not in the game". They Umpire yelled, "Batter up." Boy did things change! We started hitting the shit out of the ball and scoring runs.

Their pitcher had switched balls at the beginning of the game. Had it not been for that foul ball, that guy would have pitched a perfect game.

We won that night and eventually ended the season tied with this particular team, for first place. We never went to Douglas to pick up our Trophy.

Having coached and managed at all levels of baseball, I have seen the different personalities in players. You have to "Baby" sone of them. Others, you find yourself getting angry at them and that makes them play better. Some you have to "Suck-up" in order to have harmony in a ball club. All these include players from Pee Wee, Little League, Babe Ruth and Men's Teams.

In the lower leagues, Pee Wee and Little League, you find yourself baby sitting about 50% of the time. The kids are so immature in their thinking that you constantly have to talk Baseball to them.

There was a game, which was quite intense, when one little kid came up to me and asked if he and another boy could bet a baseball and warm up on the side lines. I looked in the direction where the two boys were supposed to be warming up. Nobody was there. I looked around and spotted them walking through the Stands, each with a snow cone in their hands... What they had done was this: the baseballs that they had taken from the Ball Bag to warm up, well, they took them to the Concession Stand and handed them over for snow cones!!! I didn't tell them anything because if I were their age, I would of even had the notion to do anything like that. Kids are smart!

One night down n Douglas, the guy scheduled to pitch that night, decided that the team he faced was too strong. I said, "Let me be the judge of that. You ARE pitching tonight. So get your ass out there and warm up." He said "OK" and started to loosen his arm. Now this particular guy is about 6'2" tall, 210 pounds, good looking as hell and built like an Adonis. In fact, we called him "Tarzan". Good body on that bastard! Anyway, he starts pitching and he's holding his own out there. About the fifth inning, in a close ball game he calls, "Time Out" and motions for me to go out to the mound. I went out there and asked, "What's up Jerry?" He answered, "You have to take me out Coach, I'm getting a blister on my pitching finger." I looked at his hand and saw some redness. I asked him, "Jerry, have you ever had a blister from pitching before?" He said, "No, I haven't" I looked at him and said, "Your coming out of the game when I tell you, not when you want to. Now, get these bastards out so we can all go home. He continued to pitch and was doing ok for a while. Then they started to hit that ball all over the Ball Park. I called, Time, went to the mound and asked to see his hand. His finger had really blistered and then broke. So, I told Jerry, "Ok kid, go sit down. Nice try." I called for our ace to mop up. We won and went home. Jerry didn't pitch for a while til the blister area on his hand healed. He was all right after that.

After the Ball Season was over, I saw him on Main Street, he said to me, "Coach, can I talk to you a minute?" I said "Ok". He said, "That night that I called Time Out when I was pitching, I used the excuse of the redness on my pitching hand just so that I could come out of the game. I got really mad at you when you told me that you would be the one to tell Me when to come out of the game. I found out, later at home why you left me in the game, and it wasn't so I could get a blister either." I told him, "You're a quick learner, Jerry, You see, I could see that you wanted out of the game because you weren't sure of yourself out there. I wanted to prove to you, that if YOU made up you mind to do something, you could! And by God...you can." He replied, "That's what I wanted o talk to you about. Thanks! You gave me confidence that night and I'll remember that experience when an uncertain situation comes up in the future. I know now how to handle it. Again, thanks Coach!"

I saw Jerry long after both of us had 'Hung up our cleats' and I could see an air of complete confidence about the man. That made me feel good!

I am an easy-going guy, I think. I make friends easily enough. I don't think I have enemies. I might have, but I am not aware of it. What I am getting at is this: When I am Managing or Coaching, I Demand 100% attention from my players. I tell them that on the Ball Field, they belong to me for at least two hours, or whatever the length of a Ball Game is. If a ball player is to do good at his position out on the field, I too want to do good whether it's Coaching or Managing. Let me illustrate what I mean when I say. I want discipline and cooperation from my players.

One night I took a Fast Pitch Softball Team to play the Fort Huachuca All-Stars. Wait! Let me begin from the beginning.

I received a letter from Special Forces at Fort Huachuca, stating that they had an All-Star Fast Pitch Team that wanted to play some games with good Teams in preparation for the All-Army Softball Tournament to be held somewhere in the near future that year and the Team wanted to be in Tournament shape by playing games with Teams they hadn't seen before. Well, I had an above average Team which won just about every game that we played. I won't have it any other way. On my Team I had four brothers. One was the Center Fielder, one the Third Baseman, one the First Baseman and the other brother was our Catcher. He was the most athletic of the four brothers. We had practices in the afternoons after we all got out of work. Some of the guys would bring a bottle or can of beer to practice. Although I didn't approve, I would tolerate it, at practice. I told the guys that I did not want anybody drinking at the Park when we had a game. They all said, "Ok". We practiced hard and with intensity for about two weeks in preparation to meet the Huachuca All-Stars. Game Day arrived. We went to Fort Huachuca in our own personal cars. I got there ahead of the Team to look up the people in charge. I made the line-up, which included the four brothers. Pretty soon, the players on our Team started to arrive.

Their players were already on the Field warming up. Our players came to the Dugout, put on their spikes and went out on the Field to loosen up their arms. Pretty soon, our Catcher arrives, Beer in hand. I didn't say anything. He put on his spikes, took a swig from the beer can and proceeded to warm up with the rest of the players. I very calmly got our Score Book and re-did our line-up, minus our Catcher and put the name of the second string Catcher in the line-up. The head Umpire came over to say that the game was to start in ten minutes. I told the guys to come in so I could call out the line-up we were to use in the game. I called out the names and positions that the guys were going to play. When it came to the Catcher's position, the name they expected to be called---- Wasn't! I took the line-up to Home Plate, listened to the Ground Rules, shook the opposing Manager's hand, we wished each other good luck and I headed to our Dugout. One of the players said to me, "The other brothers said that they are not going to play if their brother doesn't start." I very calmly got the guys together and said, "I have already handed in our line-up, but I want to hear from each individual here who wants to play! Tell me now, so I can make another line-up, otherwise the other line-up I mentioned will go out on the Field." There was absolute silence in our Dugout. I continued, "I understand that some of you say that you aren't going to play unless a certain player does. Well you all know and have been told about 'Beer' at a game, so, if you don't want to play, tell me now." Nobody spoke.

The Home Team went out on the field, the Umpire hollered, "Play Ball!" Our first batter went to bat. The whole team played well, including our second string Catcher, however, I noticed that the guys were awful quiet in the Dugout. They would talk to each other like they didn't want me to hear what they were saying. The game finally ended. We lost a very well played ball game by one run. We got in our cars and headed back home. A couple of days later, we had a League Game in our town. The Catcher came over and said, "I want to apologize for letting you and the Team down by my stupidity of bringing beer to the game. I know the rules, I should have known better." I responded, "I work hard at the place where I work. I take Managing very seriously. I hate losing. I like success, so when I Manage, I throw everything into it. I don't like to come in second best. Why should I, when first place is there to be had and shouldn't I have first place if I work hard for it? That's the way

I see it." Most people are content just to get along. Not me. If I have a position, in this case, managing a ball team, then by God, I"m going to try to achieve the top and that's 'First' place. Nine out of ten people are content with second, third, fourth or last, but then, that's them.

I can honestly say that 99% of all teams in all categories that I have managed or coached, have finished in first place. I am very proud of that fact. Anybody can finish second, anybody----but not me, because I work hard not to.

THE MISSING PRACTICE BASEBALL

Each year when the Baseball Season starts, each team starts out with one or two dozen baseballs to practice with.

One year, while coaching a Babe Ruth Team, I noticed that our practice balls were becoming fewer and fewer. I couldn't figure out why.

One night, while we were playing a scheduled game at the Warren Ball Park, one of our thirteen year old players asked if he and another boy could get a ball to play catch on the side of the Baseball Field. I gave my permission. I saw them tossing the ball to one another, but my attention then focused to the game at hand.

Now, if you have been reading what I wrote in the chapter before you will already know the answer as to why our baseballs were disappearing, but just in case you missed that part, the kids would play with them for a while then turn it in for a free snow cone! I didn't realize this till I saw those boys walking through the Grandstand, each with a snow cone in their hand!

The local league had a rule, whereby any foul ball hit out of the Park and was returned, the party that returned the ball to the Concession Stand would get a free snow cone or a free coke. Well, our two thirteen year olds were turning in scuffed up practice baseballs to the dumb high school girls there for free snow cones. This went on for almost the entire Babe Ruth Season before we found out how or why our baseballs were disappearing from our equipment bag. I have been playing baseball since before I was a teenager and well beyond adulthood and never, in my born days did I ever think of anything that these thirteen year old kids did. I never dreamed of any such thing. I guess kids nowadays are more alert than we were at that age.

THE MISSING BALL PLAYER

Our son, Chris played Pee -Wee Baseball at the age of seven. He was a small child, slight of build, with hands so small that he could hardly grip a baseball. These Pee-Wee games were played in Don Luis, on a field named Wensel Field. The starting time for the games was at four o'clock in the afternoon. I would get off work at four-thirty, come home and my wife and I would get in our car and go see our son's team play.

One day we arrived at the ball field. We parked the car just outside the right field fence. We had a good advantage point to watch the game already in progress. My wife and I could not spot our son out on the field. My wife suggested that maybe Chris did not start the game. He usually played second base and had started every game in that position. The game went on. All of a sudden the batter swings at a pitch ball and the Catcher on our son's team falls to the ground. The Coaches from both teams, the Umpires and other people rush over to the fallen player. I told my wife, "I'm going to see what happened to the Catcher and while I am there, I'll talk to Chris to see why he is not playing.

When I got to the Backstop, I got the surprise of my life! The reason our son wasn't playing second base was that HE was the Catcher that got hurt! The foul ball hit him in his Adam's Apple and knocked him out for a couple of minutes. The Coach wanted to take him out of the game, but Chris said that he was all right, so Chris stayed in the game 'til it ended.

I went back to the car. My wife asked me what had happened. I told her the Catcher had got hit with the ball, but that he was all right. She then asked, "By the way, did you see Chris?" I answered, " Yes, I saw him. HE is the Catcher."

My wife was a nervous wreck the rest of the game!

THE DUMB "KNOW IT ALL"

Our Babe Ruth Baseball Team and I were siting on the bleachers awaiting the finish of a game in progress, so that we could take the field. It was a Saturday and as we all know, Big League Games are televised on Saturdays. One of our players on our team asked if we had seen the game on TV that day and if we had seen a certain player hit a home run with the bases loaded. He asked, "You guys see the guy hit that Grand Slam?" All answered, "Yes." Sitting next to our team was a boy who played on the other team we were going to play. He asked, "What's a Grand Slam?" This guy is in his third year of Babe Ruth Baseball, lets everybody know that he knows a lot about the game, and he asked 'that' question???

One of our boys then told him it was a home run with the bases, "juiced." Well, he didn't know what "juiced" meant. It had to be explained to him.

Some of the guys thought they would have some fun with his idiot, so they made up some stuff. One said, "So and so got caught in a "pickle", (rundown). Of course, the so called "know it all", asked what a "pickle" was. The boys kept on, "Yeah, then the infield put on "the wheel play." The "know it all" was so confused with the baseball 'lingo' that he very slowly got up and left. Our guys had a ball laughing their heads off.

When the game we were watching was over, we went on the field, warmed up and proceeded to beat the other team.

TWO VERSIONS

In the days when radio was King, when there was no such thing as TV, not here in Bisbee anyway, Baseball Games were broadcast from the different Big League Ball Parks.

There was the "Game of the Week", every week. The announcer, Al Helfer, would announce the game over the air. On this particular day, the New York Yankees were playing the Washington Senators. My Mother, an avid baseball fan, would listen to the games every time they came on the radio. During one of the weekly broadcast games, Mr. Helfer was giving the Senators lineup, when all of a sudden my Mother said, "Did you hear what he just said?" I replied, "What did he say Mom?" She said, "The announcer said something in Spanish!" She answered, "Adios". I said, "Mom, the man said "Eddie Yost', he is the Shortstop." Mom just said, "Oh". Later on, as the game progressed my Mom said to me, " I didn't know the Yankees had a Mexican ball player on their team." I asked her, "Why do you say that?" She replied, "The announcer said, "now batting for New York,–'Joe Rivera'." I told my Mother, "Mom, the announcer said, 'Yogi Berra'". "Oh", was her response.

If my Mother were alive today, she would really hear some doozie Hispanic names on TV. Names like Galarraga, Martinez, Gonzalez, Alomar, Ordonez, Estelella, Encarnacion, Cedeno, Marrero, Reteria, Soriano, Garcia Parra, etc. She would turn over in her grave if she heard the Japanese names like Irabu, Nomo, Shin Jo and Ichiro.

WHEEL BARROW RACE

I was milling around after watching th annual "B Hill Climb Race", when I was approached by Mr. Manuel Lugo, one of the Bisbee Committee Members that was in charge of the Fourth of July events at Brewery Gulch. He told me that there was to be a Wheel Barrow Race and that he had acquired six wheel barrows, but that had only five "Pushers", (that's what he named the persons that would handle the wheel barrow.) Mr. Lugo wanted me to push the sixth barrow so that the race could get started. I told Mr. Lugo that I had dress clothes on, plus dress shoes with leather soles. I looked around at the other contestants. All of them were wearing Levis, tee shirts and sneakers. Mr. Lugo gave me the ol, "be a good sport", spiel. I finally said, "Okay, I"ll do it". He explained to us the route of the race. We were to start in the street, in front of one of the bars, go down to the mouth of Brewery Gulch, go in front of the Goar Building, then go back up Brewery Gulch and turn back down to the "Start Line", which was also the "Finish Line." We were to have somebody in the "barrow" as the "Rider". The "Pusher" would guide the wheel barrow down Brewery Gulch to the mouth of Brewery Gulch, where the "Rider" would 'Switch' with the "Pusher" and continue to the finish line.

I saw a young lad about 12 years old to ride in the wheel barrow, but Mr. Lugo said, "No, we want somebody that will be able to push YOU when you change places." I had to tell the kid that he couldn't be in the race after all. As I was explaining the reason to him, I spotted my brother, Ted in the crowd. He was with a girl. I asked him if he would want to be in the race as my "Rider?" He said "Yes!" I knew he would because he was the 'show off' type and this was ideal for him because this kind of thing would make an impression on the girl he was with.

The other five contestants, whom I recognized right away, were all former athletes who had played football or basketball. Besides that, they were four to five years younger than me!

The race started innocently enough, although I had trouble getting traction with my leather soled shoes. In that respect, I was at a disadvantage.

We raced to the mouth of Brewery Gulch, the "Pushers" switched places with the "Riders," however, I chose not to! My brother, Ted weighed about 160 - 165 pounds, I would say the heaviest of all the "Riders". At the time, I weighed 175 pounds. I was struggling, although I was leading the race. I chose not to switch because I was sure that Ted probably couldn't handle the wheel barrow with a 175 pound weight.

As we went in front of the Goar Building, one of the wheel barrows behind me clipped me, hitting me on my right heel. I felt blood inside my shoe and I knew the wheel barrow tore through skin on my heel. I immediately slowed down, as two of the wheel barrows passed me. That's when I got angry.

I don't like to be beaten at anything, if I can help it, because I have a lot of pride. Somehow, I picked up some inner strength and caught up with the two wheel barrows which had passed me. Apparently they heard 'foot steps', because one of the guys pushing his wheel barrow veered off toward the other hitting it. One went out of control to the left, the other went to the right and I "limped" straight down the middle to the finish line. Victorious!!

Mr. Lugo came over and gave me $50.00. The Bisbee Daily Review photographer snapped the winner's picture, me as "Pusher", Ted as the "Rider" ! I gave Ted $25.00 and started to walk home.

I looked back and my brother Ted was being hugged by the girl he was with and being congratulated by several people!! How about that? Ted, "rode"all the way, gets paid, hugged and congratulated. I, on the other hand, pushed him all the way, got hurt and had to go home to take care of my bleeding foot.

When I got home, I took off my shoe and 'bloody', wet sock. I even had blood between my toes. My shoe was soiled with blood. My heel showed a spot the size of a silver dollar where my skin was torn off from being hit by the wheel barrow, so I stayed home the rest of the day because I couldn't "walk" very well.

The next days newspaper had a picture of Ted and me and "our" winning the Wheel Barrow Race. Of course, there was no mention of the ordeal I had to go through to win the race just to satisfy one man by being a "good sport".

There has never been a Wheel Barrow Race since then, so I can safely say and proudly say, "The Winner and Still Champion.......!!

WHO ARE YOU TALKING ABOUT??

I liked Parades. When I was a child, my parents would take me, my brothers and sisters to watch the Fourth of July Parade. In those days, there used to be bands marching to the beat of military staccato music. Soldiers from Fort Huachuca would be marching in perfect and erect lines led by an officer. Behind a few floats would be the Bisbee High School Band, all dressed the same, but in civilian clothes and playing as they passed by. The music from these bands made all of us proud and alive. It really made it special day.

That was in the past. Now a days a couple of floats decorated in a patriotic motif come down, followed by pickups with Little Leaguers in their uniforms throwing candy at the crowd. Next a flat bed truck with Mariachis playing a Mexican tune. This is followed by a bunch of horses ridden by ladies and men from different horse clubs. After them, comes the Sheriff and his Posse all on horse back. Shades of the old West. Yahoo! Next, maybe the winner of the Coaster Race with his trophy and the winning coaster on a pickup passes by, along with the other Coaster Race contestants on different pickups. Phelps Dodge usually will have one or two of their humongous vehicles at the end.

To come to the point of this article, my wife and I were standing in front of the entrance to the Warren Ball Park, watching the parade go by. The Sheriff and his Posse were going by. A man, whom I knew, but will not name, said, "Look at the ass on that horse." The people in the immediate area started laughing. To this day I don't know whose "ass" the man was talking about, the horse or the rider. Hmmmm! Interesting!

POLITICS AT THE BAR

During th late 60s early 70s, there was be a United States Presidential Election. The Candidates was Richard Millhouse Nixon, the Republican nominee and John Fitzgerald Kennedy, the unanimous choice of the Democratic Party.

On this particular night, I walked into the 400 Club Bar. Most of my friends used to meet there, not necessarily to drink, but to get together and just 'hang out'. When I went in, I heard a lot of talking. One guy was asking, "Did you guys see the debate the other night between Nixon and Kennedy?" Someone responded, "I did, and Nixon looked like hell. One the other hand, Kennedy looked 'alive and fresh'. Another guy at the bar replied, "That's because Kennedy had a make-up crew to 'spruce' him up, while Nixon just came as he was and refused to be 'made-up'."

All the guys up and down the Bar were either for Nixon or for Kennedy. The discussion was getting really heated when the bartender pounded his fist, hard on the bar and in an angry voice said, "Enough with the politics! Talk about something else!" One guy directed his voice to the Bartender and asked, "what shall we talk about then?" The Bartender answered, "I don't care. Talk about sex if you like." There was silence at the bar for what seemed like the longest time then a voice from the back of the bar yelled, "Fuck Nixon!"

So you see, the conversation did turn to sex after all!

HOW ABOUT THIS ONE

The girl was a Senior at Bisbee High School. It was the beginning of the school year with the boys practicing to make the Puma Football Team. At school, a group of girls got together to form a cheerleading team. There were about 12 girls trying out for 8 positions on the Cheerleading Squad. There were girls from well to do parents as well as from poor families. Among the group was this petite, athletic, vivacious girl with a lot of enthusiasm. In fact, this girl was one of two of them that had athletic moves. The other girls that were trying out were the "dainty" type. The type that would make a big deal if they happen to chip their fingernail or scrape their knee. Some of the girls picked up the routines quite nicely, while others plodded along. This Senior girl that I'm writing about was picking up and absorbing the routines quite nicely.

After practicing for about three weeks, supervised by an adult female, the team was going to be announced. Sure enough, as school was in progress and the girls were in their respective classes, a voice blurted out through the intercom from the Principles Office, "Will the following girls please report to the Principals Office." He proceeded to mention the names of the girls. Among the names that were called was this particular girl's name. The girls all went to the office.

There, the Athletic Director named the 8 girls who were to make up the Cheerleading Squad. The Director then said that a ninth girl would be named as an 'alternate' in case, for whatever reason one of the girls could not attend a function, the alternate would take her place, till the girl got well or whatever. The ninth girl was this Senior girl I am writing about. She got up from where she was sitting and started to leave. The

Athletic Director asked her where she was going, that she was part of the group. The girl told the Director, "I tried out as a Cheerleader, I did not try out to be an alternate, so I am going back to class." The Athletic Director tried his best "snow" job on her, but it did not work. The girl went back to her class.

That afternoon when her father came home from work, he found his daughter crying in her room. She told her Dad what happened. Her Dad asked her, "Well, who 'did make the squad?" The girl named who made the team.— One was a Dentist's daughter, another girl's Father was a Justice of the Peace, another parent was a Contractor and one was a Store Owner. This girl's Father was just a worker for a local utility company, therefore, 'he' saw why his daughter hadn't been picked. Every one of these girls, (who made the Cheerleading Squad), Fathers had some kind of prestigious title in the Community. So there it was, "Preference". The Father of the disappointed girl told her it wasn't the end of the world. She eventually got over it, however, the Father didn't. You see, the Father had experienced "Preference and Prejudice," for years. This was nothing new to him, because it still exists, even in our schools. I know of what I'm talking about, because I am that girl's Father. After all, later on in life, she turned out all right.

Thank You.